Leicester**Symphony**Orchestra

The First 90 Years

Neil Crutchley

Published by
Leicester Symphony Orchestra Publishing

LeicesterSymphonyOrchestra

The First 90 Years

Neil Crutchley

First edition.
Published in 2013 by Leicester Symphony Orcestra Publishing.
69 Greengate Lane, Birstall, Leicester LE4 3JG

Photographs selected and supplied by Sam Dobson
Printed by: Ask Sue Witts
Design and artwork by Chiltz Creative Ltd, Leicester

A CIP catalogue record for this book is available from the British Library

ISBN 978-0-9575888-0-6.

Foreword by John Florance

In this marvellously informative, absorbing and well crafted book, Neil Crutchley celebrates the history of Leicester Symphony Orchestra - its ups and downs, its triumphs and stumbles. The story is related with warmth and enthusiasm, and he shows the huge role the LSO has played the cultural life of the city.

This is the story of successive generations of musicians who have been members of the rank and file of an orchestra. Their enthusiasm and talent have, down the years, made the orchestra and its achievements possible. Music lovers have great reason to be thankful to these largely anonymous musicians.

Great names stride through these pages - Sargent, of course, the founder of the Leicester Symphony Orchestra, and also such luminaries as Beatrice Harrison, Albert Coates, Henry Wood, Adrian Boult, John Barbirolli, Florence Austral, Solomon, Joseph Szigeti, John Suchet, Natalie Clein, Nicholas Daniel and Dame Evelyn Glennie…the list goes on.

There are some pleasant surprises along the way. For example, I was pleased to learn that the LSO gave the first Leicester performances of Beethoven's Ninth Symphony, Elgar's Cello Concerto and Prokofiev's Peter and the Wolf. I had no idea that the LSO played the soundtrack to the 1963 film, City of Contrasts, or that they had their own first day cover stamp issue in 1980.

The orchestra is now in fine shape and faces the future with confidence. Long may the orchestra continue to flourish. Long may this book be read. The story of the Leicester Symphony Orchestra deserves to be told.

John Florance
April 2013

Acknowledgements

My grateful thanks must go to the many people who have given me help, advice and information and without whom this book could not have been written.

I am especially indebted to the late Arthur Hames, a loyal member of the LSO for forty five years whose kindness in lending me programmes, reviews and other documentation was invaluable. It has allowed a far more comprehensive survey of the orchestra's activities in the late fifties and early sixties than would otherwise have been possible. His son Alan has continued the cooperation and has made available Arthur's papers and programmes for my use.

I am also extremely grateful to Dr Arthur Temple, a former chairman of the orchestra and a player of many years standing who has given me a great deal of information and practical help as well as hospitality and encouragement.

Special thanks must go to Pat Dobson, the present leader of the LSO's cello section and long-standing chairperson of the orchestra, for her encouragement and practical help and also to her husband Sam whose enthusiasm for the project has been an inspiration. I am also grateful to Pat's immediate predecessor, Martin Gilding, who has given so many years of service both as a horn player and a committee member.

To Robert Knight, a former manager of the LSO, I owe a debt of gratitude for his willingness to allow me access to his archive of photographs and for his many suggestions.

My thanks must also be recorded to the following people who have given me a great deal of useful information and assistance: The late Doreen Adnett, David Barclay Rhodes, the late David Belcher, Rosemary Bradshaw, Olga Briggs, Christine Bulman, Robert and David Calow, the late Kenneth Garner, the late Ruth Goldsmith, Theresa Hopkins, Judith Lord, the late Mike Raftery and the staff of the County Records Office, Neil Roberts, Kitty Stead, Terry Weston and Doreen Whitty.

Bibliography

Aldous, Richard - *Tunes of Glory, The Life of Malcolm Sargent* - Hutchinson 2001
Reid Charles - *Malcolm Sargent* - Hamish Hamilton 1968
The Leicester Mercury
The Radio Times

Author's Note

From 1984 to 2012, I was a music critic and correspondent for the Leicester Mercury. Readers should be aware that between these years, I wrote a large number of Leicester Symphony Orchestra reviews and where no attribution accompanies quotations from concert notices, they are mine.

Neil Crutchley ©

Contents

Introduction

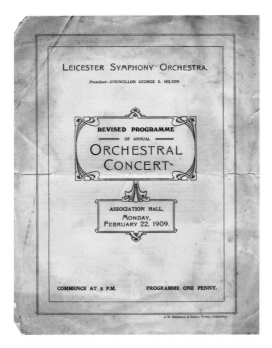

LEICESTER SYMPHONY ORCHESTRA.

President—COUNCILLOR GEORGE E. HILTON

REVISED PROGRAMME
OF ANNUAL
ORCHESTRAL CONCERT

ASSOCIATION HALL,
MONDAY,
FEBRUARY 22, 1909.

COMMENCE AT 8 P.M.   PROGRAMME ONE PENNY.

Cover of the earliest Leicester Symphony Orchestra programme held in the orchestra's archive showing that the name was used before 1922. This one dated February 22, 1909.

It could be imagined that the announcement of the formation of the Leicester Symphony Orchestra was met with cries of "Not another orchestra, we can barely support the ones we have at present". The idea of an orchestra bearing the city's name was not a new one, as a Leicester Symphony Orchestra had existed in years immediately prior to the building of the De Montfort Hall. It was originally known as the Leicester Municipal Orchestra and was formed in 1899 under the direction of Henry Ellis. Later, it was renamed the Leicester Symphony Orchestra and Ellis was succeeded by John Addison Adcock. Its president was Councillor George Hilton, a well-known figure on both the municipal and musical platforms of the town and a member of the Leicester shoe manufacturing family.

The orchestra consisted of over eighty players, "All residents of the town and county of Leicester" as the printed programmes proudly announced. Its concerts (given in the Association Hall of the YMCA) were of a fairly light nature and combined popular ballads and instrumental interludes with orchestral works. For example, in February 1912 the programme consisted of fifteen items, the most substantial of which was Haydn's Clock Symphony. The orchestra, along with all but one of Leicester's other musical institutions, did not survive the Great War.

Two decades into the twentieth century, Leicester had been given the status of a city and George Hilton was its Lord Mayor. It was recovering from the horrors of the Great War but was, as industrial cities go, a reasonably pleasant and prosperous place in which to live. It was not without poor housing, bad sanitation or crime, but in comparison with many other industrial cities of a similar size, its problems were fewer. Leicester's industries were fairly light, the goods it made much in demand and many of its companies known the world over. It had an enlightened council with a strong social conscience and a certain non-conformist piety; due no doubt, to the fact that many of its most influential members (the "city fathers" from the professional and factory owning classes) were devout Methodists, Baptists, Congregationalists and Unitarians. This long-standing association with non-conformity over several generations led to Leicester being nicknamed the Capital of Dissent.

There was plenty of culture for those who wanted it with three large and handsome theatres in the town centre and the De Montfort Hall, then acknowledged to be one of the finest concert halls in the country, set in its own landscaped grounds just off London Road and adjacent to the open spaces of Victoria Park. There were also many smaller venues and dozens of societies devoted to artistic and cultural pursuits. Of course there was no television or radio, but there were the new cinemas and these were proving very popular. High culture could be more of a problem however; audiences for De Montfort Hall concerts were inconsistent and it wasn't always the big names that attracted the largest numbers. Also it is no surprise to find less enthusiasm for contemporary music, but that applies as much today as it did then.

One thing that soon becomes obvious is that there was no shortage of musical activity in Leicester, as a glance at the Concert Announcements in the Leicester Mercury will show. Here is a sample taken from the last three months of 1920.

The Carl Rosa Opera Company (the foremost touring opera company of the day) offered three operas over the course of a week: Puccini's Tosca, Mascagni's Cavalleria Rusticana and a real novelty, Suzanna's Secret by Wolf Ferrari. These were performed at the Opera House in Silver Street, an elegant theatre demolished in 1960. A report of one of these performances sees as a sign of the times the fact that "only one man in the audience wore evening dress".

Around the same time, the Mercury was advertising "A stupendous attraction" in the form of the world renowned Diaghilev Ballet. The company was making its first appearance outside London and although Diaghilev was noted for his patronage of contemporary composers such as Stravinsky and Ravel, no chances were being taken in Leicester where the ballet on offer was Les Sylphides – an almost certain box office success.

The De Montfort Hall was the venue for a number of events including a series of Sunday concerts given by the De Montfort Orchestra under its regular conductor G R Tebbs, a pivotal figure in the development of the symphony orchestra in Leicester. These concerts were invariably well attended and it was reported that the orchestra "played with a degree of excellence for which they have become noted". As an interlude at these concerts and in recognition of the Sabbath, Victor Thomas (a popular local musician) played a selection of sacred items on the hall's fine Taylor organ.

PHOTO: COURTESY OF MRS SHIRLEY TEBBS

The photo shows G R Tebbs (centre) with his musical friends, probably about the time of the formation of his De Montfort Orchestra in 1913. Tebbs was acknowledged by all to be a crucial figure in the development of classical orchestras in Leicester. This photo shows him with his cello but he was equally at home playing trumpet, french horn or trombone.

W H Russell, a name that will figure prominently in the early years of the Leicester Symphony Orchestra, was promoting "A Grand Christmas Festival performance of Handel's Messiah". This featured over 500 performers including the Leicester Music Society and The Leicester Oriana Choir. This was the time of mammoth renderings of Messiah – the general view being the more performers involved, the better the result.

The De Montfort Hall also saw appearances by two musicians who were soon to become internationally known names: the pianist Artur Rubinstein and the violinist Jacques Thibaud. There was a recital by Madame Calve which was given to a half empty hall and prompted one commentator to suggest that "perhaps there were not enough musical people in Leicester to go round". This observation has been made many times since, although on that occasion it was probably more to do with the type of music on offer. Filling a hall seating around 3,000 for a vocal recital does seem rather a tall order.

Another name to figure prominently in the setting-up of the Leicester Symphony Orchestra was Grace Burrows. In November 1920 she was conducting a get-together ensemble in a performance of Mozart's "Prague" Symphony, which was praised by the local critic for its "clear sharp playing". She was also leading a string quartet which gave an enterprising concert for the Leicester Chamber Concert Society consisting of a string quartet by Ethel Smyth and On Wenlock Edge by Vaughan Williams. Although these modern works were well received, they drew a small audience to the Edward Wood Hall on London Road. This very grand church hall was a popular concert venue then as it is now, and since it became part of Leicester University, it has been re-named the Fraser Noble Hall.

As well as the festival Messiah, choral music was represented by a performance of Mendelssohn's Saint Paul given by the Leicester Music Society conducted by Charles Hancock.

This drew a full hall as did the Leicester Philharmonic Choir's Elgar selection coupled with A Tale of Old Japan by the once popular Samuel Coleridge-Taylor. These items were performed with what was described as a "full band".

One hundred and forty voices of the Leicester Glee and Madrigal Society conducted by Vincent Dearden, gave an evening of English madrigals with items by vocal soloists as well as instrumental pieces, which, rather surprisingly, also drew a large and appreciative audience.

Concert promotion seemed to be the province of the large music shops and piano galleries. Foremost among these at the time were Sir Herbert Marshall, founder of the Leicester Philharmonic Society and W H Russell soon to be intimately associated with the Leicester Symphony Orchestra. Both these establishments put on a series of subscription concerts. The third of the Marshall series in December 1920, a Surprise Night, saw the first appearance in Leicester of the renowned concert pianist Claudio Arrau. There was also a series of Max Mossel Concerts. These featured appearances by Margaret Balfour, Arthur de Greef and Mossel himself. Another local musical institution, Dalton's Music Shop, was promoting a Quinlan Concert Series. This included a recital by Renee Chemet – billed as "The World's Greatest Woman Violinist" and an appearance of the "famed American baritone" George Curzon.

Despite what appears to be an embarrassment of musical riches, one concert goer was prompted to write to the Leicester Mercury about the poor quality of music on offer in the city and to accuse the audiences of ignorance. He gave an instance of a recent De Montfort Hall concert where the "rather large" woman next to him spent most of the time whilst the music was being performed, "unwrapping and chewing several sticky sweets and not paying the slightest attention to what was happening on the platform". However, she applauded "with furious enthusiasm at the end". The correspondent wondered if he was alone in his cynicism.

Overall, the general picture seems to be one of a high number of concerts of variable quality. Some were well attended others were not. Karl Russell (the son of W H Russell) felt that for every successful concert in Leicester at this time, there were probably four unsuccessful ones. In view of this comment and the documentary evidence, what need was there for yet another local musical body to spread the potential concert going audience even thinner? There was already an established symphony orchestra connected with the De Montfort Hall, which seemed to enjoy a fair degree of success. What was to be gained by creating another? Very little it would seem. But that would be overlooking the promotional zeal of Karl Russell and his faith in the inspiring and charismatic young organist from St Mary's, Melton Mowbray.

1. Early Days

Some things seem destined to happen and it would not be unreasonable to argue that had Malcolm Sargent not been on the doorstep and looking to take his career a step further, the Leicester Symphony Orchestra may never have come into existence. As it was the situation could not have been better for the creation of a small piece of provincial musical history.

Harold Malcolm Watts Sargent was born on April 29, 1895, at a house in Ashford in Kent. Agnes Sargent (Malcolm's mother) had been visiting an old friend when she gave birth, rather earlier than expected, to her first child. It was not until the end of the following month that Agnes brought her baby son back to the Sargent family home, 24 Wharf Road, Stamford, Lincolnshire; a small terraced cottage just around the corner from the town's gasworks. It was here that Malcolm Sargent grew up and was to live until he was nineteen years old. His father, Henry, was a coal merchant's manager who had a strong love of music. He was the organist and choirmaster of the church of St John the Baptist in the centre of the town. It wasn't long before Henry was encouraging his young son to take an interest in music.

The rewards came quickly, as Malcolm proved to have outstanding musical ability from a very early age. With the help of his father and his piano teacher, the renowned Mrs Fanny Tinkler, he gained his Associateship of the Royal College of Organists at the age of sixteen. When only nineteen, he took his Bachelor of Music degree and was successful in fighting off the considerable competition to win the coveted post of organist and choirmaster at the beautiful church of St Mary, Melton Mowbray, Leicestershire. He quickly proved his worth and it wasn't long before members of other church congregations were rushing to St Mary's after their own services in order to catch young Sargent play his concluding voluntary. Often, in order not to disappoint, he played more than one piece and sometimes these merged into mini-recitals, thus making St Mary's the only church where the congregation actually increased after the service had ended.

It was in Melton that Sargent first learned a skill that was to make him world famous and it was one of his greatest attributes as a musician, namely the ability to inspire people to sing with confidence and conviction. His choristers loved him – whatever their age. They responded to his strong leadership with enthusiasm and reached a standard far beyond anything they felt they had achieved before. Never had the people of Melton heard a choir sing with such style and accuracy.

About a year after his arrival in Melton, Sargent became conductor of the town's choral society and he soon proved to be a very popular choice, not least with the wife of Canon Blakeney, the vicar of Melton. Mrs Blakeney was the choral society's president and a great music lover. It did not take long for her to realise that in Sargent, Melton had a musician of outstanding capabilities. Mrs Blakeney was a wealthy woman and also extremely well-connected. It was at her elegant dinner parties that Sargent got his first taste of high society – something he enjoyed for the rest of his life.

One of the works he conducted at Melton was Hiawatha's Wedding Feast, a composition that was to have considerable significance in his later career. In the 1930s Sargent's famous Hiawatha pageants at the Royal Albert Hall attracted a national audience. However, it was in Melton's Drill Hall in 1919 that he first fell in love with Coleridge-Taylor's delightful music.

Another of Sargent's achievements in Melton was the formation of an operatic society. He was both its producer and conductor. The operettas of Gilbert and Sullivan were the mainstay of the repertoire and this enabled him to develop another of his lifelong passions. Little did he know in those days in Melton that within a decade he would be conducting and recording Gilbert and Sullivan with the D'Oyly Carte Opera Company.

By 1920, Sargent's fame had spread well beyond the confines of Melton Mowbray. His performances were attracting discerning concert goers from far and wide and the list of patrons for the Melton Operatic Society included the names of most of the county gentry who lived in the vicinity of fashionable Melton and beyond. His outstanding abilities and personal qualities were also, by now, clear to everyone. He had a wonderful gift of making people feel important and that their contribution was also important. His enthusiasm and charm were infectious and it is no exaggeration to say that he made everyone around him feel glad to be alive. For the next fifty years he inspired choirs throughout the world in the same way.

Malcolm Sargent as a young man, thought to be taken around 1923.

Whilst at Melton, Sargent's career went from strength to strength. In 1919 he became England's youngest ever Doctor of Music. As with his Bachelor of Music degree, Sargent studied for his doctorate externally with Durham University. Characteristically, he completed the five year course in eighteen months. This was an astounding achievement when his other commitments are taken into consideration. He said that he managed it "by going to bed at three in the morning and getting up at eight".

This is an interesting article from the Leicester Mercury in 1982 explaining how the score of Sargent's composition "Impression" was lost and recovered in time for the 1982 concert.

Sargent — lost and found

HISTORY has repeated itself in a remarkable fashion for Leicester Symphony Orchestra which begins its diamond jubilee season in the De Montfort Hall tomorrow.

In remembrance of its first conductor, Malcolm Sargent,

The future Sir Malcolm Sargent rehearsing the Leicester Symphony Orchestra — a photograph dating from the early 20's which belongs to 82-year-old Mr. Cyril Vann of Birstall, whose father and brother were members of the orchestra. Mr. Vann was in the audience for the first concert in October, 1922.

the orchestra decided to include a Sargent composition, An Impression of a Windy Day in the programme for the concert.

This piece was first conducted by Sir Henry Wood who repeatedly asked Sargent for the score. Sargent was unable to oblige for the very good reason that, at that point he had not written a note! Eventually, the piece was composed "quickly and easily" while Sargent was on a golfing weekend at Cromer less than two weeks before the concert. It was an enormous success.

In deciding to repeat the work the orchestra took it for granted that they could locate the score. An exhaustive search through libraries and the BBC failed to locate one. When the programme was published an embarrassing situation was avoided when Peter Hinchcliffe, of the Goldsmith Library, tracked down the original in Sargent's own hand, at the Royal College of Music in London.

Nine days before the concert, music enthusiast John Knighton of Turner Rise, Oadby, went down to collect it — leaving the conductor Keith Smith and the orchestra just two rehearsal sessions in which to achieve the success Sargent enjoyed 60 years ago.

On February 3, 1921, Sir Henry Wood (founder of the famous London Promenade concerts), brought his Queen's Hall Orchestra to Leicester for a charity gala concert in aid of the blind. It was billed as one of the major social events of the season and drew a capacity audience. The programme was to include a specially commissioned work: an Allegro Impetuoso subtitled "An Impression on a Windy Day". The composer was Malcolm Sargent. The Concerts Committee had commissioned the work several months in advance, but a fortnight before the performance not a note had been written.

Sir Henry Wood was becoming impatient as he liked to prepare new works well in advance. It became clear that it was too late for him to learn the piece and declared that "whoever this young fellow is, he will have to conduct the work himself". For a confident and ambitious young musician, this was too good an opportunity to miss. "Impression" was completed and Sargent duly appeared on the De Montfort Hall rostrum – to great effect. The ovation he received held up proceedings to such an extent that Wood ordered him back to the rostrum to conduct the second half of the piece again.

This was the first of many De Montfort Hall triumphs for Sargent and on the strength of his success that night, Sir Henry invited him to conduct An Impression on a Windy Day at that year's London Promenade Concerts. This he did on October 11, 1921. As in Leicester, it was a great success with the audience and may even have sowed the seeds that led, over a quarter of a century later, to Sargent being chosen as Wood's successor as Conductor in Chief of the Proms.

Back in Leicester and just a week before Sargent's Proms début, local papers carried advertisements for a series of concerts promoted by Russell's of Leicester. They were to take place over the coming six months in the De Montfort Hall and their conductor was to be Sargent. The advertising copy (probably by Karl Russell) stated that "The Hon. Directors have been fortunate in securing the services of Dr Malcolm Sargent as their Musical Director. These concerts will give Dr Sargent every opportunity to display his undoubted genius and amazing versatility as composer, conductor, pianist and organist. The performances should be brilliant and fascinating".

Three of these concerts were given by a get together orchestra largely organised by Grace Burrows. They consisted of a Gilbert and Sullivan evening with four aspiring London soloists and a chorus from Stamford and Melton and an orchestral concert with Benno Moiseiwitch as soloist in Beethoven's "Emperor" Concerto and a performance of Elgar's Dream of Gerontius. The third in the series was given by the Halle Orchestra under Sir Hamilton Harty with Sargent as the soloist in Tchaikovsky's first Piano Concerto. By all accounts his performance was a great success and Harty is recorded as saying, "Sargent played splendidly, but I had the devil of a job to stop him conducting the orchestra as well as playing the piano". Later in that concert Sargent did conduct the Halle, in his own composition, A Night with Pan.

It was at this concert in February 1922, that a gifted schoolboy destined for greatness came into contact with Sargent. Michael Tippett (later Sir Michael) was a pupil at Stamford School where he began to show an interest in music. He, like Sargent before him, was taught by Mrs Tinkler and soon became conscious of the "slim, well dressed" conductor through his appearances at the school, where he was known as "the Young Doctor". Tippett was considering a career in music and was one of a coach party of boys from the school that went to the De Montfort Hall to hear Sargent.

This was a turning point for Tippett. It was the first time he had heard a symphony orchestra and to his delight the concert included a modern work: Ravel's Mother Goose Suite, which made a great impression on him. The concert strengthened his determination to take up a career in music. What's more, he would become a composer.

PHOTO: COURTESY OF ROBERT KNIGHT

Miss Grace Burrows, leader of the LSO. She helped to form the LSO in October 1922 and her last concert was May 1943.

Tippet's parents wrote to Sargent telling him they wished to "put Michael to music" and Sargent advised against it, citing how precarious the career of a professional musician could be. Happily his advice was ignored and Tippett entered the Royal College of Music where his tutor in the conducting class was none other than Malcolm Sargent. He went on to become one of the greatest British composers of the second half of the twentieth century.

Sir Michael renewed his association with Leicestershire when, many years later, he agreed to become patron of the Leicestershire Schools Symphony Orchestra. He took his role seriously and was greatly loved by the young musicians whose company he enjoyed. He conducted the LSSO on numerous occasions in Leicester and other English towns and cities and also on foreign visits.

Sargent's versatility and his brilliant musicianship were evident in all these performances. He was tested to the full in the final concert when he conducted a work of which he later became a supreme interpreter, Elgar's The Dream of Gerontius. He used three choirs: the Leicester Oriana, the Leicester Choral Union and the Melton Choral Society. John Coates was Gerontius, Phyllis Lett the Angel, and Horace Stevens the Priest and Angel of Agony. A well-known London professional, Charles Woodhouse, led the orchestra. The performance drew critical acclaim, with the choir's singing coming in for special praise. The Demon's Chorus was sung with a "bite and bravura that would have astonished a provincial choir of a decade earlier". Both Woodhouse and Coates were amazed at Sargent's abilities and his enthusiasm for the music. They could see that he had a tremendous gift for transmitting this fervour to his singers and players. After the performance, both these highly respected musicians, quite independently of each other, wrote to Elgar to tell him of this incredible young man in Leicester. Elgar was so impressed by their enthusiasm he made a point of contacting Sargent with a view to getting to know him.

The success of these concerts not only reflected well on Sargent, they also gave a tremendous boost to the promoters. Karl Russell was so enthusiastic about the future of orchestral music in Leicester that he decided to establish a regular series of four concerts given by a permanent local symphony orchestra with Sargent as its conductor.

Karl Russell was the son of William H Russell who, from very lowly beginnings, had built up a flourishing business as piano and music dealers. The store was known as the City Piano Saloons and was situated in London Road. Russell's main rival both in business and concert promotion was Sir Herbert Marshall, founder of the Leicester Philharmonic Society. His extensive premises were in Belvoir Street. It is said that the Russells longed to be associated with something as impressive as the Philharmonic Choir and now, with Sargent and the orchestra, they had their chance.

Dr Malcolm Sargent in the mid 1920s near the Royal Albert Hall.

Auditions began straight away with players coming from as far away as Nottingham, Rugby, Derby and Northampton. Local brass bands, orchestras, theatres and cinemas also provided a good source of recruitment. Sargent's reputation was beginning to spread across the Midlands and beyond. The leader and assistant conductor of the orchestra was to be Grace Burrows, probably the best-known instrumentalist in Leicester at that time. It was her task to assist Sargent in the choice of players and her experience and knowledge of the local situation proved invaluable. She had grown up in Leicester and came from a musical family. Her brother, Benjamin, was a nationally known teacher, organist and composer. Furthermore, as we saw in the introduction, Grace Burrows was already established as a noted conductor, violinist and teacher in her own right.

The governing body of the new orchestra consisted of Karl Russell (Hon. Secretary), Grace Burrows, Major L V Wykes, Mr Percy H Wykes and Mr C R Miles (Hon. Treasurer).

As rehearsals progressed, Sargent's qualities became more and more apparent. He showed infinite patience, nurtured wavering talent and encouraged the faint-hearted. Even seasoned players found themselves achieving far better results than they thought possible. He would spend time helping inexperienced players sort out seemingly insurmountable technical difficulties and suddenly they found they had the confidence to develop in an atmosphere of encouragement.

Sargent's enthusiasm and positive attitude had a great effect on the orchestra. One player put it this way, "The first rehearsal was a revelation, it transformed me as a player and suddenly I felt that I was a real musician. What had been impossible became possible. What was possible became almost easy". Another player recalls "Dr Malcolm really got things going and knocked us all into shape within a comparatively short time. He was a most likeable chap and I can remember him now, dashing up to the De Montfort Hall in an ancient American car. This old bus was literally

The earliest known photograph of the Leicester Symphony Orchestra taken in 1922.

held together with string. He would roar up to the entrance and would scramble out often black to the eyebrows because he had to make a repair during the journey from Melton. Even then, however, he was always immaculately turned out on the rostrum".

In the pre-concert publicity leaflet for the first season, the front page carried this announcement: "Messrs Wm H Russell and Son have withdrawn their Series of Subscription Concerts in order that the newly-formed Leicester Symphony Orchestra, under the enthusiastic and progressive Conductorship of Dr Malcolm Sargent, may have every opportunity to establish itself during the Opening Season. They therefore hope that their Subscribers will give their valued support to the series of four concerts which is being arranged by the Governing Body, and allow their names to be added to those ladies and gentlemen who have promised to become Honorary Members. They may rest assured that the series will be both brilliant and extremely interesting. Famous Artistes have been specially engaged to appear at these Concerts, and great Orchestral Works which Leicester has not yet had the opportunity of hearing will be performed".

This would appear, on the surface, to be a very magnanimous gesture by Russell but as the driving force (and, no doubt, the main financier) behind the LSO, it is hardly likely that he would have arranged a subscription series in opposition to his new project. However, there is no reason to assume that Karl Russell was anything other than absolutely certain that Sargent's Leicester Symphony Orchestra was going to be the most significant musical achievement the city had witnessed since Sir Herbert Marshall re-founded the Leicester Philharmonic Society in 1886.

The orchestra had a Reserve Fund and the list of subscribers who had promised donations was also on the front page of the leaflet. Many well known Leicester names of the time appear including Corah, Dixon, Gee, Hilton, Paget and Pickard.

The first concert took place in the De Montfort Hall on Tuesday October 24, 1922 at 8pm. Daisy Kennedy (violin) and Flora Woodman (soprano) were the guest soloists. The advertising copy reads, "This concert being the opening concert of the Leicester Symphony Orchestra, it is intended that the evening shall be a memorable and inspiring one. Dr Sargent will present an International programme, when orchestral works by English and Foreign Composers will be performed". The programme actually consisted of Wagner's overture to Die Meistersinger, Mozart's G minor Symphony No. 40, Beethoven's Violin Concerto, the Gopak from Sorochintsy Fair by Mussorgsky and Josef Holbrook's long forgotten choral tone-poem, Byron. For this last work Sargent assembled a chorus of nearly three hundred voices. There was also an optional soprano solo part, taken by Miss Woodman. She was described in the programme as "England's Famous Prima Donna" and behaved accordingly. She suggested to Sargent that he should move the conductor's rostrum to one side so that she could occupy centre stage whist performing. It is hardly surprising to find that Sargent resisted the suggestion as he was not to be outdone when it came to ensuring that he was the centre of attention. The concert finished with an encore, a Flora Woodman speciality: Swanee River sung to an accompaniment (played by Sargent on the piano) of Dvorak's Humoreske.

Press response to the concert was enthusiastic. The critic of the Leicester Mercury felt the new orchestra had made a promising start and that the players were entitled to feel encouraged by the evening's success especially as it attracted a large and enthusiastic audience.

Before going into detail about the performances he had this to say, "It would be absurd to suggest the new organisation is within reasonable distance of perfection. Good orchestras are not made so quickly. Conductor and players need further experience of each other for that to happen. In the meantime, it is shaping admirably".

There was a tendency for the players to "over run" the beat and the brass section left something to be desired. As the reviewer stated, "The greatest gulf between a local and first rate metropolitan ensemble is in the brass tone". He was impressed with the overall performance of the orchestra under its "brilliant" conductor and felt that the splendour of the Meistersinger overture was well realised although it "peaked" before the final bars. The Mozart symphony began rather ponderously but soon turned into a performance of "intimate sympathy and distinction". Holbrook's Byron was "interesting, with ideas of real value" but it was felt that the composer's "cleverness" got in the way. Flora Woodman was in good voice and Daisy Kennedy gave a "majestical" account of the Beethoven.

The Illustrated Leicester Chronicle sounded this warning, "Do not assume just because the orchestra made a good start, it will last. Other things have made equally good starts and have not continued. It is up to the people of Leicester to show a steadfast pride in the organisation, which may be regarded as the sign of a cultured community. It is a test as to whether Leicester is sufficiently advanced musically to deserve a first rate orchestra".

Having fired this warning shot, the Chronicle's critic then went on to say that the orchestra had made a triumphant first appearance with some fine performances. Like the Mercury reviewer, he also thought the brass section needed refining. Sargent was considered to be just the right man for the job being "young, of high attainments, energetic and ambitious".

The reaction in both papers could be described as "modified rapture". Probably because of a typical provincial caution, the writers seem to feel that although the orchestra had distinguished itself, local support really had to be maintained if it was to survive and prosper. As we saw in the opening chapter, Leicester audiences could be extremely fickle in their willingness to turn out for concerts, no matter who was appearing. So it is understandable that press commentators should be a little cynical about the orchestra continuing beyond the novelty of its first season.

However, by the end of the second concert, held November 28, 1922, there was a much more positive response to the orchestra's future. The Leicester Mercury critic thought it was a stage further in finding itself and that it had improved to a noticeable extent. On this occasion the conductor was Adrian Boult. Sargent was, by popular demand, to appear as the soloist in a performance of Rachmaninov's Piano Concerto No.2. The programme began with Wagner's Flying Dutchman overture which was considered to be an impressive performance with some very fine string playing. There was also significant improvement in the brass. Holst's Perfect Fool ballet music was regarded as strange in idiom but skilful and expressive. It was admirably realised. Sargent's playing of the Rachmaninov was described as "a personal triumph" and a performance of "the utmost brilliance". There was a sensitive accompaniment from the orchestra. After the concert, Boult who was described in the publicity leaflet as "The world famous conductor of the British Symphony Orchestra", declared the LSO to be, "Well on the way to becoming one of the very foremost of provincial orchestras".

By the third concert, held February 22, 1923, there was an almost ecstatic response from the press. The Leicester Mercury reported that everything went miraculously right for the orchestra. "Here is an organisation that has been in existence for less than six months and is already well on the way to that blend of perfect coherence and mutual understanding adhered to technical mastery". Sargent began the concert with a repeat performance of his own Impression on a Windy Day and this set the standard for the whole evening. The music was described as having "a charm of its own combined with skill of construction and high spirits".

The world famous composer and pianist Ferrucio Busoni was to have been the guest soloist but was indisposed. His place was taken by Mitja Nikisch who played Liszt's Piano Concerto in E flat. The main item was Tchaikovsky's Fourth Symphony and here the orchestra really came into its own in a performance that did the piece full justice.

The final concert of the season, held April 19, 1923, was billed as an "English Composers' Festival Concert". The De Montfort Hall was to be specially decorated for the occasion and Sir Henry Wood came from London as the guest of honour. The soloist was Dorothy Silk who was described as "the brilliant soprano". She was making her first appearance in the city. The pre-season publicity handbill states:

"An extremely interesting English Musical Programme will be given at this Concert, commencing with the early English Composers and concluding with the latest developments of modern Orchestral Composition. It is hoped that at this concert the Leicester Symphony Orchestra will have the honour to introduce to Leicester the Choral Work of a famous British Composer which has aroused so much discussion in musical circles, "THE HYMN OF JESUS" (Holst)."

Sargent, with hallmark carnation, conducting the LSO in the De Montfort Hall in the early 1920s

The day after the concert, the long headline for the review in the Leicester Mercury proclaimed "Symphony Orchestra in Some Striking Examples. Seal Set On Growing Reputation. Large Audience Filled With Enthusiasm". The critic questioned the judgement of putting The Hymn of Jesus at the end of the concert but he did think it was a masterpiece despite its difficulties. Mars, Venus and Jupiter from Holst's Planets Suite were also played and Jupiter proved so popular it had to be repeated. The early music is not mentioned but Dorothy Silk distinguished herself in two songs with orchestra by Granville Bantock: The Lament of Isis and By the Ganges. Sargent was given the credit for the "immense advance in the skill of the orchestra".

The orchestra's Governing Body felt the first season had been a success and that Sargent had excelled himself. They realised that he was their greatest asset and was well on the way to becoming the idol of musical Leicester. Karl Russell was also delighted with the season and had good reason to be proud of his own judgement in choosing Sargent to conduct his new orchestra. The results spoke for themselves.

Looking back over the music performed, there is no doubt that some of it must have been tremendously taxing for a new and relatively inexperienced orchestra. It is worth remembering

L.S.O. TRIBUTE.

At the Leicester Symphony Orchestra's rehearsal on Sunday, the conductor, Dr. Sargent, paid a tribute to the noble work that the late Mr. Tebbs had done for orchestral music in Leicester, as conductor of the De Montfort Hall Orchestra. He said that whatever position the L.S.O. orchestral music in Leicester might attain in the future, it should be remembered that to Mr. Tebbs was owing a great debt of gratitude, in that he realised the great possibilities of orchestral music in Leicester.

The orchestra standing, Dr. Sargent read the following:—"We, the members of the L.S.O., at this our first meeting since the lamented death of Mr. G. R. Tebbs (conductor of the De Montfort Hall Orchestra) hasten to pay our tribute of profound respect to the memory of one who for so long fostered the cause of orchestral music in this city. We deeply regret the departing of a fellow musician, and mourn the loss of a personal friend. We tender our sincerest sympathy to his family, and all whom he held dear to him, and in all Christian reverence trust that our loss may be his gain."

PHOTO: COURTESY OF MRS SHIRLEY TEBBS

Malcolm Sargent pays tribute to G R Tebbs at the time of his death in 1923. The title of the orchestra is mis-quoted as it should not include the word "hall".

that in 1923, the Perfect Fool ballet, the Planets and the Hymn of Jesus were new and unusual works. Their idiom was by no means familiar. Even today players find them difficult, but in 1923 they must have seemed terrifying. There were no recordings or broadcasts in those days and it is almost certain that the vast majority of the players would not have been familiar with the music. They would have had to learn all the tricky rhythms and meters from scratch and if the performances were as good as the reports suggest, it says a great deal for Sargent's talents as an orchestral trainer.

A sad note was sounded in December 1923 when George R Tebbs, the conductor of the De Montfort Orchestra, died at the relatively early age of fifty two. Tebbs was a prominent local musician who believed passionately in bringing good orchestral music to a wider public. He began as a trumpeter with the Wesley Hall Orchestra and then became its conductor. It was this ensemble that formed the nucleus of the De Montfort Orchestra, which performed in the new concert hall from the year it was built. A number of the players in Tebbs's orchestra were also in the pre-war Leicester Symphony Orchestra before it was disbanded.

Before the next rehearsal of the LSO, Sargent paid a generous tribute to George Tebbs, saying, "Whatever position the Leicester Symphony Orchestra and orchestral music might attain in the future it must be remembered that Mr Tebbs was owed a great debt of gratitude in that he realised the great possibilities of orchestral music in Leicester". The De Montfort Orchestra was eventually disbanded.

Not surprisingly, Karl Russell was pleased with the orchestra's achievements and promoted the second season with great vigour. He was rewarded with full houses and gratifying box office returns. The first concert got things off to an excellent start. It consisted mostly of Wagner excerpts including the Tannhauser Overture which, in the critic's view, was played with "crystal clarity". Madame Carrie Tubb (soprano) and Robert Radford (bass) were the guest artists and they each sang a group of popular songs including Sea Fever and O Star of Eve. The headline in the Leicester Mercury said it all, "Brilliant Playing In Wagner Evening. A Very Successful Send-Off To The Second Season - Full House".

One of Sargent's early admirers was his friend and contemporary, Herbert Howells. Howells was making a name for himself as a composer of distinctive style and imagination, as shown in his colourful orchestral showpiece Procession. Well read in Slavic literature, Howells dreamed one night that he was in a Russian city where a great religious procession was coming towards him with menacing tread and flamboyant music. On waking the composer found that he had total recall of the music in his dream and wrote it down without hesitation. This formed the basis of Procession, which was completed in full score within the week.

Sargent heard Procession at the Proms and was impressed. In fact the piece was such a success that it had to be repeated before the concert could proceed. The following morning Sargent told Howells that he intended to perform Procession in Leicester and invited him to the De Montfort Hall to hear it.

That concert proved to be a highlight of the second season. Along with Procession, the programme included Schubert's Great C Major Symphony and Haydn's Cello Concerto played by the glamorous Portuguese cellist Guilhermina Suggia.

Suggia and Howells travelled to Leicester on the same train, having met at the booking office, where they also fell in with a small, well-built man, smoking a pipe. He was buying a ticket in broken English and he too was carrying a cello. Suggia, surprised and delighted in equal measure, recognised him as her old teacher Pablo Casals, regarded at the time as the world's greatest cellist.

Casals was going to Manchester by the same train and the three musicians shared a compartment. Suggia was overjoyed. They said farewell to Casals at Leicester and on the way to the De Montfort Hall she turned to Howells and said, "Tonight I shall play like a goddess." True to her word, she even looked like a goddess: swathed in a geranium red gown, her majestic profile displayed to striking effect. The audience was enraptured. However, it is also recorded that in the midst of such glamour: "Malcolm held his own, not to be outshone."

The highlight of the season was to be a performance of Beethoven's Ninth Symphony on March 6, 1924, Leicester's first. Sargent rehearsed his forces with incredible intensity. Some years later he said of this performance that his amalgamated choir was good, his orchestra less so, but the emotional impact of the music and the audience's tremendous response left him in such a highly charged state that he locked himself away in the lavatory. He did not want to speak to anyone, as he wasn't sure that he would be able to control his feelings. This was a remarkably uncharacteristic gesture for Sargent, who was normally so gregarious.

The performance was viewed locally as a truly memorable occasion. The Leicester Mercury was in no doubt: "Triumph For Dr Sargent And His Orchestra" was its headline. Once the critic had got over his understandable incredulity that Leicester had had to wait a hundred years to hear Beethoven's Ninth, he praised the performance saying that it was even finer than he thought it would be. There was a "crowded, appreciative and attentive audience" and despite a bit of scrappiness in the strings, the standard of playing and singing was high. The soloists were: Elsie Suddaby, Clara Serena, Ifor Thomas and Arthur Cranmer, the latter being especially impressive in his opening exhortation. "Malcolm Sargent and his performers are to be greatly congratulated" he concluded.

The season ended with a further performance of Elgar's Dream of Gerontius. Another capacity audience was treated to singing of "remarkable beauty and power" from the combined forces of the Leicester Choral Union and the Melton Mowbray Choral Society. The orchestra came in for rather more restrained praise, but Sargent shone as expected.

By the end of the second season, there was no doubt that the Leicester Symphony Orchestra had established itself as one of the city's most successful and fashionable musical institutions. With its many talented players, a gifted, elegant and articulate young conductor and a large and distinguished following, the future looked bright.

2. *Growing Fame*

By the time it had reached its third season, the Leicester Symphony Orchestra was beginning to build a reputation beyond the borders of the county. One result of this was that it started to attract the attention of some extremely distinguished musicians. The first of the season's concerts featured three guests, or at least, two and one by proxy. There was Jelly D'Arranyi in Saint-Saens' B minor Violin Concerto, Tudor Davies in excerpts from Hugh the Drover by Vaughan Williams and Myra Hess in the form of an "Aeolian Duo Art Pianola", playing the first movement of Grieg's Piano Concerto.

This novel idea came from Karl Russell and was really an advertisement for the latest type of player piano, which reproduced the performances of great artists in the home. Paderewski, Grainger and Alfred Cortot were amongst those who had recorded for Aeolian. Not surprisingly,

This Russell advert from the October 1924 concert programme includes the Duo-Art piano.

Russell had a stock of Duo Art player pianos in his shop. Myra Hess, who had played the Grieg Concerto in Leicester only a few months earlier, had recorded the solo part of the concerto for demonstration purposes. Russell thought it would be an unusual and no doubt lucrative idea to feature the Duo Art player piano at an LSO concert. He paid handsomely for the privilege by donating, at Sargent's suggestion, a hundred pounds to the orchestral fund.

Russell was no fool when it came to publicity. He was a stylish entrepreneur who made sure that his own business (the City Piano Saloon) was featured in a full-page advertisement in every LSO programme. Every one of these advertisements was a work of art and carefully scripted to make it quite clear that in Leicester, there was only one place to buy pianos and that

One of the many and varied Russell adverts of the period. This one from the 1928-1929 season brochure.

was Russell's. The December 1925 programme proclaims that "Great names in music lend lustre to the Russell reputation", and from the programme of March 22,1928: "Our fine wares are the world's finest pianos". In October 1929 a "Russell Reverie" comprised four paragraphs of praise for both Leicester and the Russell family and ends with the slogan, "Russells - Leicester's chief Ministers of Melody". In March 1933 concert goers were invited to visit "the finest collection of world-famous makes of piano ever assembled under one roof". Naturally, these eye-catching advertisements stopped when Russell withdrew his patronage and they were replaced with a similar type of thing extolling the virtues of Bosworth's piano and music stores on London Road, Allen Bosworth being the orchestra's librarian and a long serving member of the LSO's cello section.

A well known story is told of the rehearsal for the Grieg concerto with the player piano. Sargent was instructed to conduct the orchestra with his right hand, and to cue the piano by pressing an electric switch held in his left hand. The piano was wheeled onto the platform before the rehearsal began and the two electric leads were connected – or so it seemed. One lead went to a socket backstage and the other to Sargent's desk, where it was connected to a cue button which allowed the conductor to bring in the piano at the right moment.

The first item to be rehearsed was Schubert's Unfinished Symphony. The Andante was well into its stride when to everyone's surprise and amazement the piano burst into life and a deafening cascade of chords shattered the serenity of the Schubert. Grieg's Piano Concerto had started of its own accord. Try as he might, Sargent could not stop the machine. He frantically pressed his button but this had no effect. Then it stopped and everyone thought that was that but it was merely a tacit section in the score and sure enough, at the appropriate moment, the piano began again. Players stared in incredulity as the machine ploughed on, its keys moving of their own accord. Someone tried to attack the control mechanism but to no avail. Suddenly and for no obvious reason it stopped. It was later discovered that Sargent's cue button had not

THE ORCHESTRA

VIOLINS

Miss Grace Burrows
(1st Leader)
Mr. F. Muston
(2nd Leader)
Miss E. Adcock
Miss M. Ashmell
Mr. Van Baelen
Miss C. Blockley
Miss M. Brown
Miss C. Dearden
Miss E. H. Ellis
Mr. H. Gilbert
Mrs. H. Gilbert
Mr. W. Hall
Mr. R. J. Holt
Miss Humberstone
Miss G. Jewsbury
Miss L. Loseby
Mr. B. Moore
Miss M. Mortimer
Mr. L. G. Mansfield
Mr. W. G. Page
Miss D. Peck
Mr. H. Petts.
Miss D. A. R. Potts
Miss M. Raistrick
Mr. R. Rudd
Mr. H. Vann

VIOLAS

Mr. T. Kienle
Mr. C. Garratt
Mr. R. E. Getliffe
Mr. F. Glover
Mr. P. W. Neale
Miss E. Raiment
Mr. J. H. Vann
Mr. A. H. Bass

VIOLONCELLOS

Mrs. C. Robertson
Mr. K. A. Holyoake
Mr. W. A. George
Mr. C. H. Mansfield
Miss P. New
Mr. T. A. Sharpe
Mr. C. Woodford

CONTRA BASSO

Mr. F. T. Dawson
Mr. A. S. Kirkham
Mr. H. Matthews
Mr. A Matthews
Mr. G. Simpson
Mr. G. Ward

FLUTES

Mr. F. Dyson
Mr. J. H. Kinton

PICCOLO

Mrs. L. Ackroyd

OBOES

Mr. J. Oldershaw
Mr. A. H. Bradbury
Mr. P. W. Powell

CLARINETS

Mr. A. V. Palmer
Mr. F. L. Islip
Mr. H. Malkin

BASSOONS

Mr. H. W. Bird
Mr. J. W. Brown

HORNS

Mr. K. E. Winkless
Mr. W. S. Simmons
Mr. H. Hyde
Mr. T. Bent

TRUMPETS

Mr. S. S. H. Iliffe
Mr. W. Hillier

TROMBONES

Mr. C. Iliffe
Mr. A. E. Smith
Mr. H. Whitmore

TUBA

Mr. H. Rainbow

TYMPANI

Mr. L. G. Collis

PERCUSSION

Mr. G. F. Hardcastle
Mr. F. Gilbert
Mr. E. E. Jackson

HARPS

Mr. A. E. Shipley
Miss G. Kilbourne

LSO player list from the October 23, 1924 programme. Note, Miss M Ashmell is Mary Thornley's maiden name. She was 14 when she joined, having been spotted by Grace Burrows, her violin teacher.

been connected and a backstage electrician had accidentally activated the piano. However, on the night, everything went smoothly and at the end of the performance, Sargent pretended to shake hands with the invisible Myra Hess. The demonstration had proved to be a great success and Russell was very pleased with his idea – and his subsequent sales of Duo-Art pianos.

One of England's leading pianists Harold Samuel appeared at the concert in December 1924 and, as befitted a Bach specialist, he played that composer's D minor concerto. This was, according to the advance publicity, "in response to very many requests". The major orchestral works were Elgar's Enigma Variations and oddly, just the the first and fourth sections of Rimsky-Korsakov's Symphonic Suite, Scheherazade. In the tradition of the day a selection of popular ballads was included in the programme and these were sung by a promising young baritone named John Goss.

Cover of programme from 1 February 1925.

The concert of February 5, 1925 saw the appearance of two outstanding figures: the cellist, Beatrice Harrison and the composer and pianist, John Ireland. Either one of these artists would have been enough to draw the crowds; to get both at the same concert was an extraordinary achievement. The publicity stated: "The first visit to Leicester and exclusive appearance at this concert of these two World Renowned Artists will mark an epoch in the musical history of Leicester, and has already aroused great interest in local musical circles". Beatrice Harrison played the Elgar Cello Concerto – its first performance in Leicester and Ireland played some of his piano pieces and conducted his impressionistic tone poem, The Forgotten Rite.

The Leicester Mercury's critic had this to say about John Ireland, "Most people pass through a period of intense dislike of Mr Ireland's music, before realising there is "something in it" and proceed then, by easy stages, to disciple". He regarded the innocuous Forgotten Rite as "a difficult nut to crack" but conceded it showed a "high quality of musical imagination". In the Elgar, he saw a work of greatness with no hint of "fuzziness" about it. "It bears in every bar the stamp of lofty thought" he stated and conceded that Beatrice Harrison played with "high imagination", although her "unvarying tremolo had a monotony of effect".

The orchestra had made considerable strides and its skills were tested to the utmost in Strauss's Till Eulenspiegel. The players came near to "doing it full justice". However it was in Mendelssohn's Midsummer Night's Dream Overture that the best playing was heard and the performance was described as a "high water mark". The whole concert was described as "a triumph for the personality of Dr Sargent as conductor".

DE MONTFORT HALL - LEICESTER

THURSDAY, 5th FEBRUARY, 1925, at 8 o'clock

THE EVENT OF THE LEICESTER MUSICAL SEASON !

THE LEICESTER SYMPHONY ORCHESTRA

(70 INSTRUMENTALISTS).

Conductor :

DR. MALCOLM SARGENT

Exclusive Engagement and First Appearance in Leicester !

BEATRICE HARRISON

The World-Famous English 'Cellist.

Miss Beatrice Harrison will be associated with the Orchestra in the First Performance in Leicester of the ELGAR VIOLONCELLO CONCERTO.

Exclusive Engagement and First Appearance in Leicester !

JOHN IRELAND

The Famous Composer and Pianist.

Great interest will be created in the first appearance in Leicester of Mr. John Ireland, known throughout Great Britain as the Composer of "Sea-Fever" and many other charming Songs and delightful Orchestral and Piano Compositions.

Mr. Ireland, in addition to conducting the first performance in Leicester of his own Orchestral Work "THE FORGOTTEN RITE," will by special request of local Music-Lovers, play a group of his Piano Compositions.

THE ORCHESTRAL ITEMS will include the First Performance in Leicester of

Tone Poem, "Till Eulenspiegel" ("Till's Merry Pranks")—*Strauss*

and also

The Overture to "A Midsummer Night's Dream" (Mendelssohn) and The Overture to "Sarka" (Smetana).

Doors open to Ticket Holders at 7-10.   Ordinary Doors at 7-30   Seats cannot be reserved for Ticket Holders after 7-30.

Reserved Seats (Including Tax)	Balcony	7/6 & 5/9	Unreserved (Including Tax)	Stalls	2/-
,,	,, Grand Tier	5/- & 3/6	,,	,, Gallery	1/6
,,	,, Stalls	5/- 3/- 2/4	,,	,, Promenade	1/-

A Special Late Concert Train will leave Leicester (L.M.S.) at 10-40 p.m. for Syston, Brooksby, Asfordby, Melton Mowbray, Oakham and Stamford.

Secure your Seats at once from

WM. H. RUSSELL & SON
THE CITY PIANO SALONS
LEICESTER   Tel. 475

P.T.O.

Concert poster from February 5, 1925, one of the most prized items in the LSO archive. Note the reference to the special late train that had been organised.

22

At the March concert Beethoven's Symphony No. 3 "Eroica" was sandwiched between Brahms' Second Piano Concerto and a Chopin nocturne. Ivan Phillipowsky was the soloist. Other works in this enormously long evening included Bach's Brandenburg Concerto No.3 and an aria from the same composer's Cantata No. 151 sung by Dorothy Silk, who also sang the almost inevitable group of popular vocal items. The whole thing was rounded off with the orchestra playing two of Brahms' Hungarian Dances.

Once again, the LSO had experienced a successful season both artistically and commercially, although there was a feeling in some quarters that the programmes were rather too adventurous. In an article in the Leicester Mercury on February 7, 1925, an announcement was made about the setting up of a trust fund "to enable the work of the LSO to be carried forward and to provide first-class orchestral music in Leicester". An anonymous donor had given a hundred pounds to start it off. This was followed by what sounds almost like an assurance: "Next season the orchestra will make itself more accessible, with less emphasis on advanced orchestral novelties. Each concert will contain a standard work which will enable all classes of music lover to judge of its quality".

Whether this change in policy was brought about by strong public opinion or by the players themselves is not clear. The "advanced orchestral novelties" were works that Sargent liked and he kept most of them in his repertoire throughout his career. However, from the non-professional player's point of view, learning all this new music on top of a full time job, was very tiring, even though it was exciting. Also, although the audiences had not been a cause for concern, there was now room for improvement and more works from the standard repertoire could do the trick. As it turned out, the fickle Leicester audience was not entirely swayed by these efforts as the first concert of the fourth season proved.

Two outstanding artists were booked to appear and the main orchestral work was Beethoven's Fifth Symphony, so on the face of it, this event should have been a sure-fire winner with a capacity house. The great French pianist Alfred Cortot came to play both the Schumann Concerto and Cesar Franck's Symphonic Variations, while Dame Ethel Smyth, that most formidable of lady composers, appeared to conduct her overture The Boatswain's Mate. Sargent conducted Rimsky-Korsakov's Capriccio Espagnole as well as the Beethoven symphony.

Understandably, the critic in the Leicester Mercury thought Cortot was the highlight of a very good evening. In Schumann's Concerto the playing was "masterful" with the soloist giving "added meaning to every passage". Ethel Smyth was credited with "showing that good orchestral thinking is not an exclusively masculine province" and Sargent conducted a "sparkling and piquant" account of the Capriccio. In the Beethoven, the orchestra sounded rather tired but gave an eloquent performance nonetheless with Sargent showing "a good sense of architecture and proportion".

However, before all these compliments, the critic gave this warning: "If Leicester is to continue having its own symphony orchestra under the conductorship of a musician of international repute, it will have to provide a larger audience than the one gathered for its opening concert of the season."

This is the first of a series of comments about disappointing audiences that have run like a litany through critics' reports on the orchestra almost up to the present time. There is often a sense of bewilderment on the part of the commentator, as there seems to be no obvious reason for the fluctuations in audience numbers. It can happen when the orchestra plays popular works and when they have world famous guest soloists. At other times, for seemingly lesser events, the audience is an unaccountably large one. By all reasoning, the above concert should have attracted a full house. Cortot was undoubtedly one of the greatest concert pianists of the day and he was playing popular works. Ethel Smyth was a much-loved character as well as a fine composer and conductor and should have proved an added attraction. As if that were not enough, the orchestra was playing the most popular of Beethoven's symphonies. Even the personality of Sargent (who had just been appointed as the conductor of the British National Opera Company) did not always work its magic.

The season continued with appearances from two more internationally renowned artists, Florence Austral, the famous Wagnerian soprano and the glamorous Portuguese cellist Guilhermina Suggia. This evening took the form of a "concert – recital" with piano accompaniment, as Sargent was elsewhere. An announcement in the programme stated, "The best wishes of our audience will be extended this evening to our esteemed conductor, Dr Malcolm Sargent who, by special invitation is conducting the Royal Philharmonic Society, Queen's Hall, London".

A Centenary Concert marking the death of Beethoven was the highlight of 1927. It was a remarkably long programme and not all the music was by Beethoven. His Egmont Overture, Eighth Symphony and

Concert - Recital

L·S·O

DE MONTFORT HALL, LEICESTER
3RD DECEMBER
1925

Concert programme cover from the Concert-Recital of December 3, 1925. This is the earliest programme to show an LSO logo.

Leonora Overture No.3 were played alongside Dvorak's Cello Concerto with Gaspar Cassado as soloist. Cassado also performed a group of novelty items with piano accompaniment.

As the 1920s drew to a close, Sargent's outstanding talent and enthusiasm had come to the notice of a wide range of music promoters. He had moved to London, where he taught at the Royal College of Music. He soon became one of the most sought after musicians in the capital and established himself as the country's leading exponent of Gilbert and Sullivan's Savoy Operas. He made many appearances with the D'Oyly Carte Opera Company and by 1930 he had recorded The Yeoman of the Guard, The Pirates of Penzance, Iolanthe, HMS Pinafore and Patience. Furthermore, Sargent was chosen by the British National Opera Company to conduct the first production of Vaughan Williams' Hugh the Drover and to follow this with a recording. He was appointed as the conductor of the Royal Choral Society, the Robert Mayer Children's Concerts and the Courtauld-Sargent Concerts, in which he conducted both the London Symphony and London Philharmonic orchestras. He was as successful on a social level and found himself courted by many a society hostess. Even members of the Royal Family came in to his circle.

Happily, none of this affected his loyalty to the Leicester Symphony Orchestra which continued to see as much of him as ever. In the 1929-1930 season he conducted all four concerts. In October 1929 he conducted Elgar's 1st Symphony. In the December concert he gave the same composer's rarely-heard Polonia and Bruch's G minor Violin Concerto with the renowned Albert Sammons as soloist. The celebrated bass, Norman Allin was the guest in January 1930 and in March Cortot was back to play Grieg's Piano Concerto. This concert also included Borodin's Polovtsian Dances and Stravinsky's Firebird Suite.

As a parallel to his children's concerts in London, Sargent set up a similar venture in Leicester. These took place on Saturday mornings and proved to be very popular with local schoolchildren. One of those present on these occasions remembers Sargent's charming and easy manner on the platform. "He put everyone at their ease and called us young ladies and young gentlemen.

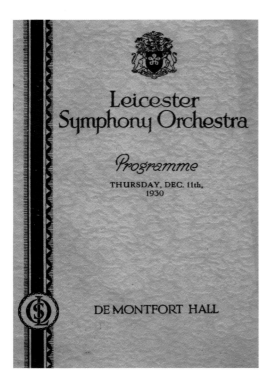

Concert programme cover from 11 December 1930. Note the change of LSO logo.

Then he would tell us stories about the music he was going to conduct and would sometimes illustrate bits on the piano or with the orchestra. He made us think of the words "how lovely the sea is" for the opening of Mendelssohn's Fingal's Cave Overture and brought to life the mischievous antics of Till Eulenspiegel and tragic love story of Romeo and Juliet. He really did begin my lifelong love of good music."

The celebrated Wagnerian soprano, Florence Austral was the soloist in the first concert of the 1932 season. Austral was the wife of the Anglo-Russian conductor Albert Coates who was soon to play a significant role in the life of the LSO. Her programme consisted of excerpts from Wagner's operas and concluded with the Liebestod from Tristan and Isolde. Leon Goossens performed in his brother Eugene's Oboe Concerto at the December concert and in February 1933 another world-renowned pianist, Artur Schnabel, appeared with the orchestra in both Mozart's B Flat Major Concerto and Beethoven's "Emperor". The prospectus for this season of concerts proudly proclaimed that this was "The Greatest Combination of International Artists Ever Brought to Leicester". It was no exaggeration.

Elsewhere Sargent was gaining a reputation as a conductor of rare gifts. He had been chosen by Sir Thomas Beecham to conduct the first performance of Walton's spectacular oratorio Belshazzar's Feast. Some say that Beecham took one look at Walton's difficult score with its irregular rhythms and dissonant harmonies and thought it would never come off so he decided to offload the work onto Sargent who by then had a national reputation as a superb choir trainer. To say that Sargent scored a success with Belshazzar would be an understatement. At the first performance, which took place at the Leeds Triennial Festival in 1931, he galvanised his forces to give a electrifying account that was met with a tremendous ovation and which completely overshadowed everything else in that year's festival. One critic wrote: "This was a great performance of a work that bears the indubitable stamp of greatness".

If Beecham had been calculating in his actions, then it had backfired. Even though he often encouraged Sargent in his early years and probably thought that by handing him "Belshazzar" he would be helping the younger conductor whilst making life easier for himself, the likelihood is that he never expected such a result. A success on this scale must have caused Beecham some discomfort, especially as he had assured Walton that he could put a couple of brass bands in the scoring if he wished (which the composer did) as "it will never be heard again". History has proved him to be quite wrong as Belshazzar turned out to be one of the most popular choral works of the twentieth century – no little thanks to Sargent, who subsequently made it one of his specialities.

In London, Sargent was in the limelight (literally) for his part in the great Hiawatha Pageants held in the Royal Albert Hall. The idea of turning Samuel Coleridge-Taylor's three-part choral setting of Longfellow's epic poem about Red Indian life into a grand opera belonged to the

Leicester Symphony Orchestra

VIOLINS:
Miss Grace Burrows
(1st Leader)
Mr. F. Muston
(2nd Leader)
Miss E. Adcock
Miss M. Ashmell
Miss C. M. Blockley
Miss M. Bown
Mr. E. Busby
Mrs. Cooper
Miss M. Cook
Miss E. H. Ellis
Miss J. Farnsworth
Mrs. C. Foss
Mrs. Kenneth Green
Miss M. Groocock
Mr. W. G. Hall
Miss M. Harris
Miss Humberstone
Mr. Keeling
Mr. Lindsey
Miss L. Loseby
Miss J. Maddison
Miss M. Mortimer
Mr. F. Mountney
Miss Mountney
Mrs. Neal
Mr. H. Petts
Miss D. Potts
Mr. R. Rudd
Miss H. Richmond
Mrs. Shea
Miss Ursula Smyth
Mr. John Taylor
Miss H. Timpson
Mr. B. V. Walker
Miss Ward
Mr. Leavins

VIOLAS:
Mr. Theo Kienle
Mr. A. H. Bass
Mr. E. Getliffe
Mr. P. W. Neale
Mr. L. Needham
Mr. A. J. de Reygheri
Miss Raiment
Miss C. M. Vergette
Mr. A. E. Shipley
Miss D. Barnes

VIOLONCELLOS:
Mrs. Robertson
Mr. A. Bosworth
Mrs. Bryce
Mr. W. A. George
Mr. K. A. Holyoake

VIOLONCELLOS—contd.
Mr. H. F. Hopkins
Mr. C. Mansfield
Mr. C. Leake
Mr. C. Woodford
Miss A. Hays

CONTRA BASSI
Mr. F. T. Dawson
Mr. F. Dixey
Mr. A. Matthews
Mr. G. G. Simpson
Mr. E. Ward

FLUTES:
Mr. F. Dyson
Mr. J. H. Kinton
Major R. P. Shea

PICCOLO:
Mr. L. W. Cullen

OBOES:
Mr. S. Pratt
Mr. H. W. Tharp

CLARINETS:
Mr. A. V. Palmer
Mr. F. L. Islip

BASSOONS:
Mr. H. W. Bird
Major L. V. Wykes
Mr. C. L. Wykes

HORNS:
Mr. K. E. Winkless
Mr. G. Baker
Mr. F. W. Hyde
Mr. W. E. Simmons
Mr. C. A. Wilkes

TRUMPETS:
Mr. S. S. H. Iliffe
Mr. E. Moore
Mr. H. Wykes

TROMBONES:
Mr. D. G. Burdett
Mr. G. Adcock
Mr. J. B. Smith

TUBA:
Mr. Morris

HARP:
Mr. A. E. Shipley

TYMPANI:
Mr. L. G. Collis

PERCUSSION:
Mr. G. F. Hardcastle
Mr. H. A. Westley
Mr. F. Allt
Mr. H. W. Britcher

At the Piano—Dr. BEN BURROWS

LSO player list from the December 15, 1932 programme.

producer, Thomas Fairbairn. He felt it would make a wonderful spectacle in a large theatre with a cast of hundreds. The arena in the Royal Albert Hall was ideal. The production had its first run in 1924 and was tremendously popular. It was repeated the following year. Originally the conductor had been Eugene Goossens with Sargent as his associate, but Goossens left to take up the conductorship of an American orchestra, so Sargent took over the baton and very quickly made the Hiawatha pageants his own. They ran for several years and became a highlight of London's musical calendar.

Sargent's achievements elsewhere only served to enhance his reputation and influence in Leicester, where by 1932, Hiawatha pageants were being held in the De Montfort Hall. Sargent's friend and well-known local musician Victor Thomas had seen the London production and had been so impressed that he formed a society in Leicester for the purpose of giving similar pageant style opera performances. Needless to say the first of these was to be Hiawatha. With the help of Thomas Fairbairn as producer, a real Red Indian Chief as the Medicine Man, a huge chorus and the Leicester Symphony Orchestra, he was able to emulate Sargent's metropolitan success. Thomas's Leicester Choral and Dramatic Society gave annual pageant operas in the De Montfort Hall for the next twenty five years.

By the age of thirty eight, Sargent was well on the way to an international career. He was a sought after artist in both the concert hall and the recording studio and he was equally sought after as a guest at fashionable parties. London society had taken to him in a big way and he would frequently dance the night away" before taking an early morning rehearsal and then crossing London for an afternoon recording session followed by an evening concert or a Hiawatha performance. None of this social activity affected his work, but it may have been a contributing factor in the near fatal illness that was creeping up on him.

3. Shock Waves

By the spring of 1932 friends were beginning to comment on Sargent's appearance. Sartorially he was as immaculate as ever but he was looking thinner and also rather sallow. One member of the LSO commented that "he was lively and charming – no change there, but he was as thin as a rake and looked ill. We were beginning to get concerned, but there was no point in saying anything because he was - or at least seemed, so full of energy. Anyway, he wouldn't have listened to any of us as he was obviously leading a charmed and very glamorous life by then. Who could blame him for making the most of it? We were very lucky to have him in Leicester".

At first his Leicester players were unaware that he had been experiencing spasms of severe pain but when he collapsed during the interval of the first of that year's Royal Albert Hall Hiawatha performances it was clear that something was wrong. However, he appeared to recover and his life continued at the same hectic pace. But this was the calm before the storm, as by March 1933 he was in severe abdominal pain and confined to his bed with a fever. A diagnosis was made and it was not encouraging. A tubercular abscess had been found and an immediate operation was essential. It was touch and go. Happily the operation was a success but the recovery period was a long one. He was out of circulation for well over a year.

The concert scheduled for March 16, 1933 was billed as a "Modern Composers' Festival Concert" and included two Sargent specialities, Holst's Perfect Fool ballet music and Constant Lambert's 1920s jazz-inspired choral classic The Rio Grande. Lambert was due to appear at the concert to conduct his own work and Sargent was going to play the piano part. As it turned out, Lambert

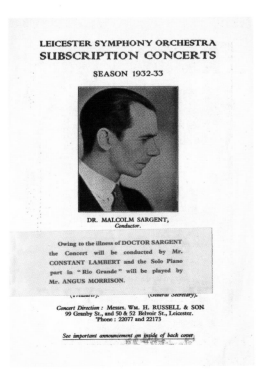

The red note in the programme of March 16, 1933 sets alarm bells ringing.

conducted the entire concert and Angus Morrison stood in for Sargent on the piano. This solved the problem for one concert but what was going to happen for the rest of the year?

Sargent's illness was one of two severe blows the Leicester Symphony Orchestra received that season. The other was the withdrawal of Russell's patronage. It was rumoured that Karl Russell felt that his business was not getting enough glory from its association with the orchestra. A more likely reason is that times were hard and the company could no longer afford to underwrite the costs of the orchestra and the fees of international soloists. Whatever the real cause of Russell's withdrawal, it put the orchestra in a very difficult position. Quite simply, it would have to disband unless it could become self-supporting.

Fortunately the orchestra's ever-resourceful oboist Arthur Thornley had just been made its Honorary Secretary and he went to visit the convalescing Sargent at his London home to discuss the situation. From his sick bed Sargent arranged for Thornley to meet the well-known concert promoter Harold Holt. The outcome was the temporary amalgamation of Holt's International Celebrity Subscription Concerts (which at that time were an established part of many a large town's concert season) with the concerts of the Leicester Symphony Orchestra. The guest conductor was Albert Coates who was to become a favourite with both the orchestra and its audience, although box office returns were slow to recognise this and for his first concert, an all Wagner evening, there were many empty seats.

Sargent's illness was causing problems elsewhere. He had been invited to Australia to set up a symphony orchestra for the purpose of broadcasting. This project had to be put on hold for three years. His work in London which included children's concerts, the D'Oyly Carte Opera Company, the Royal Choral Society and the Hiawatha pageants, was divided between nine other conductors including Sir Thomas Beecham, Sir Adrian Boult and Sir Hamilton Harty. Planned recordings had to be rescheduled and artists rebooked.

All this rearranging gives some idea of Sargent's workload and his importance to the country's musical life. Yet somehow he found the strength during his darkest hours to secure a deal with Thornley and Holt to save his Leicester Symphony Orchestra.

4. Two Societies Combine

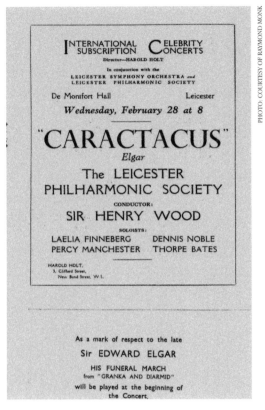

PHOTO: COURTESY OF RAYMOND MONK

Cover of concert programme February 28, 1934. This was just five days after Elgar's death.

The amalgamation of the Leicester Symphony Orchestra concerts with those of Holt's International Celebrity Series was a success from the orchestra's point of view as it offered a lifeline. Unfortunately it was less successful on a commercial level and it appears that Holt did not wish to extend the arrangement beyond that initial season. In fact, within the space of another year, Leicester did not have a Harold Holt International Subscription Series or any other subscription series for that matter. So another way of supporting the LSO and of providing the city with orchestral music had to be found.

The solution came with the decision to merge the concerts of Leicester's leading choir, the Philharmonic, with those of the Leicester Symphony Orchestra under the baton of the now recovered Malcolm Sargent. A joint committee was formed and the new venture produced four concerts each season, one of which would be purely orchestral. Sometimes the Melton Mowbray Choral Society was also included in the scheme, thus providing a huge choir capable of performing the largest choral works in the repertoire. Not surprisingly Sargent was in his element with this arrangement. He was never happier than when conducting great choral works and this would now be possible at his Leicester Symphony Orchestra concerts.

The most popular events of this collaboration were the annual performances of Handel's Messiah which, under Sargent, were described by the critic in the Leicester Evening Mail as

This photo from 1935 belongs to the era when Leicester Symphony Orchestra and the Leicester Philharmonic Choir combined under the name of Leicester Philharmonic Concerts.

"sublime in every way". He went on to add, "Dr Sargent can inspire singers as no other baton can". The publicity for these performances proudly boasts of a choir of four hundred and fifty singers and full symphony orchestra! This must have raised serious accommodation problems for the stage manager at the De Montfort Hall.

Other choral works given during this time included Samuel Coleridge-Taylor's A Tale of Old Japan, Verdi's Te Deum from his Four Sacred Pieces, A Sea Symphony by Vaughan Williams, the finale to act two of Verdi's Aida and another all Wagner evening. With Sargent's reputation as a choral conductor, the greatest British singers of the day were regular visitors to the De Montfort Hall. In the 1936-1937 season these included Isobel Baillie, Gladys Ripley, Astra Desmond, Heddle Nash and Roy Henderson.

In the concert of October 10, 1935, Sargent appeared as the piano soloist and the baton was handed to the orchestra's leader Grace Burrows. As a fine conductor in her own right she was singled out for her delicate handling of the accompaniment to Mozart's Concerto in A major. Sargent, however, is rebuked by the critic of the Leicester Evening Mail for creating "a slight jerk in the process of appreciation when he made his first entry noticeably faster than the tempo originally adopted by the conductor".

Sargent was back on the rostrum for Dvorak's New World Symphony which despite some "shaky entries" achieved "an appropriate sense of bigness and energy". It was another huge programme which also included a group of vocal items from the well-known contralto Mary Jarred, accompanied on the piano by Dr Ben Burrows. A note in the programme read, "Owing to the length of the concert no encores will be allowed in part 1".

The Leicester Mercury women's page regarded the evening as a success for the ladies and its headline read "Women's Triumph". The female artists "stood out in last night's performance - Miss Burrows of course not only for her conducting but as leader and particularly for her playing of a certain melody pianissimo in the Dvorak symphony, Miss Jarred particularly for her rendering of Che Faro from Orpheus and the encore, Where'er You Walk and, last but by no means least, Miss Elliott whose work on the cor anglais was a sheer delight".

The writer also had a lot to say about the social aspects of the concert:

"The audience was a particularly smart affair for what was probably the first social event of the season. Practically the whole of the circle was in evening dress and in the front row I noticed the Lord Mayor and Lady Mayoress of Leicester who were honouring the concert with an official visit. Everyone seemed to know everybody else and there was a large number of young people

Concert programme cover bearing the Sargent hands design by E Fairhurst, about whom no details are known.

The reverse of the same programme mentions special bus services, five different routes, laid on for patrons.

accompanied by their parents, many of the debs looked particularly attractive in their graceful evening gowns underneath their long fur coats."

One of the purely orchestral concerts early in 1937 featured a now forgotten girl violinist, Guila Bustabo, who gave what was regarded as a tremendous performance of Beethoven's Violin Concerto which prompted an unusually frank and forthright review from LS in the Leicester Mercury. It began, "Recalled again and again by an audience so enraptured by playing of supreme quality that even Dr Malcolm Sargent was for the moment forgotten. Guila Bustabo last night gave Leicester its greatest night of violin music since Kreisler played the Bach Chaconne and Fugue. This young player has the same magic around her as haloes all the great exponents of great music". He goes on to praise her magnificent playing in Chausson's Poeme and then remarked that, "It was no surprise to find the remainder of the concert failed to rise half-way to the heights attained in the concerto". The symphony was Tchaikovsky's Pathetique which was described as "patchy" and the critic suggests the lack of strong string tone may be " because of the preponderance of women players". There were times when "the strings were weak and scratchy, the brass strident, the horns dolefully suggestive of asthmatic lions".

At the end of his review LS makes another interesting comment which is worth quoting in full. "The size of last night's audience indicated a revival of interest in instrumental music and provided a pointer which the organisers should not ignore. The fusion of the Philharmonic and Symphony Orchestra has had the tendency to reduce the number of concerts given exclusively by the orchestra and last night's performance was, and will be, the only purely orchestral night of the season. This cannot be satisfactory to everybody. Choral works do not enjoy the popularity of even ten years ago. Oratorio has declined and difficulty is inevitably experienced in selecting other works of popular appeal. On the other hand, orchestral music still provides a vast field for future exploration. The Symphony Orchestra has great potentialities always provided that every effort is made to increase their strength and to secure – and this is not always the case – adequate rehearsal."

This may have prompted the committee of the LSO to think a little more carefully about their collaboration with the Leicester Philharmonic Choir and perhaps may have had some bearing on their willingness to pull out of the agreement after what seems, in retrospect, to have been a storm in a teacup.

5. Fall Out With The Phil

The joint concerts with the Leicester Philharmonic Society came to an end after just two seasons. No one could doubt their artistic success but financial disagreement between the two committees became insurmountable and the co-operation was ended.

The dispute arose over payments to a number of professional musicians in the orchestra. In a report on the disagreement in the Leicester Evening Mail of April 26, 1937, Arthur Thornley outlined the argument and said the initial agreement between the two groups was a simple one. "The orchestra were to be responsible for the entire loss on any orchestral concert and bear half the loss in any choral concert. The present position of tension had arisen because the Philharmonic Society could not agree that the payment to the orchestra's professional members for rehearsals should be included in the profit and loss account for the concert.

"The committee of the Philharmonic Society had put forward a suggestion that the concerts should be continued on the following terms – the LSO to be entirely responsible for any loss on orchestral concerts, the Philharmonic to guarantee full professional fees on Messiah and half fees on the other two choral concerts. All rehearsal fees to be cut out. This suggestion would have been impossible and placed an unfair burden of responsibility for the financial side on the orchestra."

Thornley is also quoted as saying, "the bone of contention is the payment for rehearsals, as an amateur society they (the Philharmonic) cannot understand that. They want to commit suicide and bring a verdict of manslaughter against the LSO".

These are strong words but, on the face of it, Thornley does have a point. The orchestra, although rather vague about it at times, has always paid the few professional players it engages and this is quite reasonable. The odd thing about this whole affair is that the payment of players does not appear to have been discussed when the two groups began their joint concerts.

This was not the end of the matter. A month later, the Philharmonic Society held their annual meeting and "allegations were made that the action of the Leicester Symphony Orchestra in severing the association of three years had come as a bombshell to the Society's committee who were under the impression that an agreement had been reached between the two bodies".

It appears that although the discussions between the two committees had not been particularly fruitful, the Philharmonic contingent somehow thought a compromise had been reached. But after the annual meeting of the LSO, a press statement was issued saying that a unanimous decision had been taken to sever the connection with the Philharmonic. It began, "The LSO regrets that it is unable to accept the proposals suggested by a joint sub-committee of the LSO and the Philharmonic Society concerning the financial arrangements for a further series of joint concerts. It also regrets that alternative proposals made by the officers of the LSO have been unacceptable to the Philharmonic Society's Committee".

PHOTO: COURTESY OF THE BBC

Sargent from his BBC series Talking About Music. This photo is from the 1936-1937 brochure.

Mr E Astill, who was the chairman of the Philharmonic's annual meeting, said the Society had received a letter from the orchestra severing the connection between the two societies after a joint committee had sat for three and a half hours and thought they had come to an amicable arrangement for next season. "The letter was a thunderbolt to our committee," he said.

In response to this statement, Arthur Thornley claimed that it should not have come as a surprise to the committee, as a week before the LSO's decision was made, another letter had been sent to the Philharmonic Society stating that although they did not accept the Philharmonic's proposal, the orchestra suggested in a further proposal, "that the choir should not be required to contribute anything towards losses on concerts until ALL orchestral rehearsal expenses had been removed from concert accounts. Thus ensuring the Philharmonic Society would not be saddled with the cost of three or four rehearsals". Thornley could only conclude that Astill and his committee were not fully acquainted with the contents of the letter. Had they been, he was sure that "they might have regarded it as a genuine, if not generous offer to solve the problem". Finally, he states, "if any member of the Philharmonic Society or any other interested persons would like to have further information, they may inspect all correspondence etc. (including a carbon copy of the letter referred to above) at Messrs Bosworth's, 130 London Road".

There seems to have been a lot of indignation and misunderstanding on both sides. The choir's meeting became heated and pointed questions were asked. The main bone of contention was the loss of Sargent for choral concerts. Many of those present felt that, whatever the cause of the dispute, the Phil would be the loser in any split. One questioner wanted to know why the Society had not been informed of the problems until then. He demanded to know why the letter from the LSO containing the second proposal had remained unanswered, as he felt that something could have been salvaged to the mutual benefit of the two societies. He was strongly supported in these questions by others at the meeting. The chairman reiterated his previous comments about rehearsal fees and the cost to the society. It was claimed that under the original LSO proposal, the cost to the Philharmonic would have been an additional £80 or £90 per season which would have resulted in inevitable increase in subscriptions. This account was accepted as reasonable by the meeting. However, there was still no satisfactory explanation about the lack of response to the second LSO proposal and those present were not entirely satisfied that everything possible had been done to sort out the problem.

In new arrangements following the breakdown, The Philharmonic Choir concerts were to be conducted by Leslie Heward who would bring his City of Birmingham Orchestra with him. Heward was a highly respected conductor who had been with the Birmingham orchestra since 1930. He was a musician of great insight and integrity but he lacked Sargent's charisma. It was felt that efforts should be made to patch up any disagreements between the two societies rather than lose Sargent who was, after all, on the doorstep and without doubt the most popular choral conductor in the country. It was also considered a pity to have to import an orchestra when Leicester had one of its own. Perhaps the LSO felt it was better off on its own, bearing in mind the comments made by the Leicester Mercury's critic concerning the joint concerts.

This dispute attracted a considerable amount of public interest. Letters to the press suggested various solutions including the setting up of a professional municipal orchestra under Sargent with a choral section consisting of "the best of the Phil" as its nucleus. This would ensure the Philharmonic was not deprived of the services of "one of England's greatest musical conductors". Another correspondent felt the Parks Committee of the City Council should "offer more engagements to the two societies combined" as a way of ensuring their continued co-operation. However, nothing came of these suggestions and no mutually satisfactory solution was found. So choir and orchestra went their separate ways.

Sargent's views on the dispute are unknown. By this time he was probably too busy with his blossoming international career to become involved with the general running of the Leicester Symphony Orchestra. Consequently, not for the first time (or the last), it fell to the indomitable Arthur Thornley to defend its honour.

6. Successful Seasons

Once the dust had settled over the dispute with the Leicester Philharmonic Society, the orchestra announced its plans for the 1937-1938 season. In the Leicester Evening Mail of October 26, 1937, the grandiose announcement at the top of the LSO's advertisement read, "The Leicester Symphony Orchestra will present a series of three orchestral concerts in the De Montfort Hall conducted by Dr MALCOLM SARGENT at each of which the full orchestra of 80 performers will be supported by Artists of INTERNATIONAL CELEBRITY fame".

The decision to discontinue the arrangement with the Philharmonic was referred to in the LSO concert prospectus for the 1937-1938 season. It began, "There is already ample evidence to indicate that the LSO's decision to present an independent series of orchestral concerts during this coming winter has been generally welcomed by Leicester music lovers. Whilst the amalgamation of Leicester's two principal musical organisations had much to commend it, the necessity of including three major choral works in a series of four concerts made it impossible to cater adequately for the ever increasing demand for orchestral music".

Photograph of Sargent and the LSO in 1937. It's an exceptional picture for its degree of clarity.

The Leicester Symphony Orchestra

VIOLINS :

Miss Grace Burrows
  (*Leader—1st Violins*)
Miss C. M. Blockley
  (*Leader—2nd Violins*)
Miss Edith Adcock
Mr. L. Birkett
Miss G. V. Bowen
Miss M. Bown
Mr. E. Busby
Miss I. Chamberlain
Miss M. Cooke
Mrs. G. Cooper
Mrs. Kenneth Cowan
Mrs. George Foss
Mrs. K. M. Greer
Miss M. Groocock
Mr. W. G. Hall
Mr. Thomas Keeling
Miss Cicely Kibart
Mr. Theo. J. Klee
Mr. E. G. Law
Mr. John Lindsay
Miss L. Loseby
Miss J. K. Maddison
Miss Joyce Mountney
Mr. Frederick Mountney
Mrs. P. W. Neale
Mrs. A. W. Pooley
Miss H. Richmond
Mr. Reginald Rudd
Mr. Robert Silvester
Miss Ursula Smyth
Miss Madge Stafford
Mrs. M. Stead
Mrs. Arthur Thornley

VIOLAS :

Mr. Frank W. Muston
Miss Louise Atherton

VIOLAS—*cont*.

Miss Dorothy Barnes
Mr. A. H. Bass
Mr. Kenneth Essex
Mr. R. E. Getliffe
Mr. P. W. Neale
Mr. A. J. de Reyghère
Miss Hope Timpson

VIOLONCELLOS :

Mrs. R. L. Robertson
Mr. Allen Bosworth
Mrs. M. S. Bryce
Mr. W. A. George
Mr. K. A. Holyoake
Mr. H. F. Hopkins
Mr. C. H. Mansfield
Miss A. de Reyghère
Miss P. Russell

BASSES :

Mr. Fred. T. Dawson
Mr. W. Crossley Allen
Mr. Henry H. Dixey
Mr. A. Matthews
Mr. Geo. H. Simpson
Mr. E. J. Ward

FLUTES :

Mr. F. Dyson
Mr. J. H. Kinton

PICCOLO :

Mr. C. W. Quarmby

OBOES :

Miss Caine
Mr. H. W. Tharp

CLARINETS :

Mr. A. V. Palmer
Mr. J. H. Malkin

BASS CLARINET :

Mr. S. R. Kenworthy-
  Browne

BASSOONS :

Mr. H. W. Bird
Mr. C. Wykes

HORNS :

Mr. K. E. Winkless
Mr. W. E. Simmons
Mr. F. W. Hyde
Mr. G. H. Baker

TRUMPETS :

Mr. S. S. H. Iliffe
Mr. E. C. Moore
Mr. R. Tillyard

TROMBONES :

Mr. D. G. Burditt
Mr. L. J. Tyers
Mr. J. B. Smith

TUBA :

Mr. A. E. Morris

TIMPANI :

Mr. L. G. Collis

PERCUSSION :

Mr. H. A. Westley

LSO player list from the February 1937 concert programme. Note that Mary Thornley is shown as Mrs Arthur Thornley, having married Arthur in 1933.

The first concert, held on November 25, 1937, saw Sargent conducting the first performance in Leicester of Berlioz's Symphonie Fantastique – one hundred and seven years after it was written. Other works included Faure's Pavane, The Merry Wives of Windsor Overture and Ravel's Bolero. This last item was, as the press announcement stated, "by special request". Dino Borgioli, billed as "the world-famous Italian tenor", was the guest soloist and he sang a selection of operatic arias.

The concert was a sell-out and heralded the most successful two seasons in the orchestra's history. Press reception was very favourable with the critic of the Leicester Mercury telling his readers that although it was "an unsettled question" as to whether Berlioz could be considered a great composer, his music was certainly "emotionally vivid" and he was sure that "no more interesting musical personality ever lived". The performance of the Symphonie Fantastique was judged to be a fine one with just a few ragged edges and lots of excitement. The timpanist came in for special praise for his thunderclaps in the Scene aux Champs. In Ravel's Bolero, the orchestra was chided for over reacting to Sargent's intensity too quickly by anticipating the climax and thus having nothing left in reserve for the ending.

The critic opened his review by stating: "To have to wait in a queue to get into the De Montfort Hall balcony was an experience that reminded one of the old days of music in Leicester. Whatever the cause - and I hope it is a renewed interest in real as opposed to "canned" music that is the motive force - the Leicester Symphony Orchestra started its season magnificently with a "sold out" balcony and a manifestation of public interest which must encourage it to do better than ever before."

The critic of the Evening Mail led with an ecstatic appreciation of Dino Borgioli. He declared that the audience who filled the hall, "would rarely hear a tenor who has so many of the qualities of true greatness. There is music in every note – and how the man SINGS, a lingering beauty in every phrase, a warm colour and a top note...which has ringing in it all the thrill and passion of every romantic opera ever written". Later in the review, he describes Berlioz as "a wizard of the orchestra" and claimed that Sargent and his orchestra "soared triumphantly over the impressive obstacles built by Berlioz". Unlike his colleague on the Mercury, he felt the Bolero "was worked up in great style to a dizzying crescendo".

Suzanne Harrison of the Evening Mail's women's page commented on the pleasure of seeing a full house for the concert and added, "almost the whole of the circle was in evening dress which contributed to the brilliance of the affair". There followed lengthy descriptions of the bouquets and evening gowns along with an interview with Signor Borgioli's English wife. She said looking after her husband was like looking after a racehorse. She "makes sure he does not get into draughts and does not stay up too late". The piece finished with some comments from Sargent who said he would always be grateful to the Leicester Symphony Orchestra, as it was the first orchestra of its kind he ever conducted. He would be at their service to conduct them as long as they wanted him and commented that the orchestra, "have given me the opportunity to go as far as I have".

At a civic reception after the concert, Sargent was reported as saying he did not agree with the fashionable notion of concerts becoming extinct in the provinces. In fact, he held the opposite view and cited the last four concerts he had conducted; they had all been sold out -

including that evening's. He looked forward to a time when the corporation of all large towns would stand behind their orchestras as part of the service to the municipality. He then went on to say he would like a concert such as the one they had just heard, to be given twice - once for the well-to-do who could afford good prices and one at sixpence and a shilling for those who could not. "The leisure of thinking people" he added "is a serious thing and corporations do not provide much for their leisure. It is no use regretting what people are doing unless you can give them something else to do. Music seems so necessary in this crazy world today, and a municipally-supported orchestra would not cost too much."

Reference was made to the split with the Philharmonic in a speech by the vice-president of the orchestra. He said that although agreeing to differ, the two societies remained on the best of terms. This was followed by a number of tributes paid to the work done by Arthur Thornley in promoting the success of the orchestra and for his tireless efforts on its behalf.

Benno Moiseiwitch was the soloist at the second concert and this featured another first performance in Leicester. This time it was Rachmaninov's Rhapsody on a Theme of Paganini – the most recent work by this composer. It was received, as was the soloist, with great enthusiasm. In 1938, Rachmaninov was best known for his Prelude in C sharp minor. The days of regular performances of his symphonies or any of his piano concertos, other than the second, were well into the future. So Leicester's reception of the Rhapsody was very encouraging for both the composer and soloist.

According to the Leicester Evening Mail the orchestra got off to a slightly shaky start in the Carnival Romain overture but played Schubert's Rosamunde music "as it deserves to be played, with sweetness and affection" and came through its performance of Dvorak's G major symphony "with flying colours".

There were many young people in the audience and their response to Sargent's "magnetic personality" won them over to such a degree that their applause seemed "almost personal". This sort of comment is a recurring theme throughout Sargent's time in Leicester. The headline in the Leicester Mercury read "Leicester Symphony Concert Sold Out. Orchestra surpasses itself to commemorate the occasion".

Another large audience heard the third concert on March 24, 1938. The soloist was a thirteen year old cellist, Aubrey Ranier. He played Haydn's D major concerto which the Mercury critic found a stylish reading despite a small tone and a few slips. Beethoven's Egmont Overture was a little unsteady at first but rose to a fine climax. Delius's Irmelin Prelude was "the high-water mark" of the concert and it was "quite beautifully realised" while the rather "stagey" Scheherazade by Rimsky-Korsakov was felt to be a generally fine performance despite some raggedness. Grace Burrows received a special mention for her solos as she gave "an eloquent and persuasive voice to the story-telling sultana".

The first three items of the above concert were repeated in a broadcast by Sargent and the orchestra on the BBC Midland Region Service a few days later. In fact radio broadcasting was becoming a regular event for the LSO. On July 3, September 5, 1937, and January 1, the following year, the orchestra had featured in broadcasts on the Midland Region performing works given at De Montfort Hall concerts. The Radio Times ran a short article in June 1937, headed "Drilled by Sargent" and it read: "The Leicester Symphony Orchestra now in its fifteenth year, will give a programme from the studio on Saturday 3 July. Dr Malcolm Sargent, who has been its musical director since its foundation, will conduct. Using only local material, about half of it amateur, he has produced a really fine orchestral ensemble."

Due to his increasing international workload, Sargent was not always available for these events so the New Year broadcast was conducted by Leslie Heward and September's by Reginald Burston. In a long-forgotten topical column in the Leicester Mercury called "Round the Clock Tower" by "Old John", the writer was pleased to note that "the BBC is recognising the existence of the city and county a little more in its output".

At the annual meeting of the LSO held April 24, 1938, the treasurer Mr F L Islip gave one of the most encouraging financial statements in the history of the orchestra. An overall net profit of £27 8s 11d was made over the three concerts and ninety per cent of the full fees payable to professionals would be met. Over the three previous seasons it had never been possible to pay professionals more than seventy five per cent. Arthur Thornley told the meeting that audiences had been the largest on record for the LSO and subscribers were "well satisfied with the quality of music provided". It had also been necessary to extend the special accommodation at a nominal charge of 6d per seat, as the demand had been so great. The committee was re-elected and thanks were recorded to Baroness Ravensdale, the orchestra's president, and Mr. Gorham Gee for defraying part of the cost of the soloist's fees. The local press was also commended for their interest in the orchestra's activities.

The success continued in the 1938-1939 season. Sargent was on a tour of Australia for the first concert and once again his place was taken by Albert Coates. The programme consisted of Glinka's overture A Life for the Tsar, Tchaikovsky's Fourth Symphony and excerpts from Wagner's Gotterdammerung, with Florence Austral as Brunnhilde who was, at that time, one of the greatest of Wagner singers.

The critic of the Evening Mail observed that the hour's worth of Wagner demanded as much concentration and endurance from the orchestra as it did from the soloist. He said the artists "put in some heroic work" and described their efforts as "magnificent" but said very little about the playing of the orchestral items other than noting the orchestra's size was increased to one hundred musicians. He concluded his review with the rather enigmatic sentence, "On the whole a concert of little light relief but great fascination". The Mercury's critic was sure that the

Advert from November 1938 concert programme.

orchestra's contribution in the Wagner "must rank as some of the best things they have done yet". He liked the performance of the symphony and described the strings in the third movement as "superlative". He felt the brass section was still not quite as good "as we have a right to expect".

One of Britain's most widely acclaimed pianists, Solomon, was the guest soloist in the second concert and he played the Tchaikovsky 1st Concerto and a group of Chopin pieces. Sargent began the concert with Berlioz's Benvenuto Cellini overture and ended it with the Enigma Variations. There was another full house.

Sargent was welcomed back with great enthusiasm and the orchestral contribution throughout the concert was thought to be "first class". However enthusiasm for the orchestra paled in comparison to the rapture Solomon's playing inspired. His "perfect control and effortless ease" made his Chopin pieces the highlight of the concert for CAT in the Leicester Mercury. The Leicester Evening Mail's critic LS, thought the orchestra was really gaining in confidence and experience through frequent performances and commented that the Enigma Variations was "surely and bravely played". He thought Solomon's playing "most brilliant".

Features in both local papers reported at length on Sargent's huge success on his Australian tour. He gave twenty four concerts and not only was each one a sell-out, but they were all broadcast across the continent. He also found the time to give five children's concerts and to form a national orchestra consisting of one hundred of the country's best players. This band gave three concerts under his baton and such was the success of these that after each one he was mobbed and police had to make a way for his car.

Financial help for the orchestra came from the Carnegie United Kingdom Trustees. It had not been eligible for a grant from this trust before, as it was regarded as "an organisation of national importance and prestige" and the trust was designed for smaller amateur societies such as the Leicester Bach Choir which had been the recipient of a grant. However, due to a change in the trust's policy, it now included "a limited number of large urban societies which render invaluable service to musicians generally throughout their areas". Thus the orchestra was offered financial assistance for the season in a novel way. "For every £1 raised locally in excess of last season's total income, it will receive a grant of £1 up to a maximum of £75."

The final concert of the season on March 2, 1939 was, by all accounts, the most successful. The soloist was the great violinist, Joseph Szigeti and he played the Brahms concerto. Sargent led the orchestra in Wagner's Flying Dutchman overture, Delius's On Hearing the First Cuckoo in Spring, Beethoven's 8th Symphony, and the Hungarian March by Berlioz.

The concert created a lot of press attention both before and after the event. There was a real sense of optimism that Leicester could attract world class artists to play with Sargent's LSO and that this in its turn attracted a very large and appreciative audience. There was also great enthusiasm for the new financial assistance and, particularly in the women's pages, a feeling that the orchestra and its conductor gave the city an impressive social standing in artistic circles. Sargent was always able to give glamour and distinction to musical occasions and this could have very positive results – particularly on the financial side.

Szigeti's playing of the Brahms was unanimously thought to have "scaled the heights" and the orchestra rose to the occasion with great style. CAT described the Beethoven symphony as "a jolly business" and felt the orchestra played it well. He thought the Delius "delicious" with conductor and orchestra at their very best. LS thought the Delius "charmingly played" but felt the overture to be less good. CAT had no reservations and thought it "went very well".

There can be little doubt that these concerts must have been the high water mark of the orchestra's life. Full houses, the world's leading soloists and a conductor coveted by many a professional band, made the Leicester Symphony Orchestra an ensemble of enviable stature in those immediate pre-war days.

7. War Years

The 1939-1940 season was going to be the most ambitious in the orchestra's history. Everyone was full of enthusiasm following the success of the previous two years and felt the LSO was going from strength to strength. Financially things were so good that, for the first time for many years, full fees were paid to the professional members and the accounts for the 1938-1939 season were closed with a credit balance of £138.

In fact optimism was so high that a four-concert season was planned. However, Sargent would be on another Australian tour for the first two concerts so replacements had to be found. In October his place was to be taken by Sir Adrian Boult who was, at that time, conductor of the BBC Symphony Orchestra and for the November concert, none other than the great Sir Henry Wood, founder of the Proms would conduct. International soloists were to include Albert Sammons (violin), Clifford Curzon (piano), Guilhermina Suggia (cello), and Egon Petri (piano).

That two of the most distinguished conductors of the day and a host of international celebrity soloists were prepared to come to Leicester is quite remarkable and says a great deal for the reputation of the orchestra and its conductor at that time. Of course, by now Sargent was internationally known and in great demand. He had just taken over the Halle Orchestra and was making guest appearances with virtually every orchestra and choral society in the land. He was also making more and more appearances overseas. When all these factors are taken into consideration, it is clear that the Leicester Symphony Orchestra had been very fortunate to retain his services for so long. However, there were no illusions on the part of the orchestra's committee. They could see that it was only a matter of time before the pressures of international celebrity forced him to relinquish his regular appearances with his first orchestra.

Sadly, due to the outbreak of war, the first two concerts were cancelled and the LSO's first appearance that season was on Sunday March 11, 1940. This was an afternoon concert and was rather sparsely attended. It led the Mercury's music critic to suggest that when it came to a choice between a symphony concert and an afternoon snooze, most Leicester music lovers chose a snooze. But he goes on to say that the LSO "came out like giants" for Sargent in a programme that included Dvorak's Carnival Overture, Delius's A Song Before Sunrise, Rachmaninov's Second Piano Concerto (played "supremely well" by Clifford Curzon) and Cesar Franck's Symphony in D minor.

There was some concern over the small attendance at this concert but the committee decided to go ahead with another event. It was billed as a "Summer Concert" and was to be held on Thursday May 23, 1940. Prior to the concert, Arthur Thornley was quoted in the Leicester Mercury on the subject of the orchestra's future. He said, "This concert will be a decisive factor in determining whether the LSO shall disband for the duration of the war. The orchestra has small financial reserves and cannot risk them further". Commentators in both the Mail and the Mercury felt it would be a sad loss to the city if the orchestra disbanded and urged Leicester's music lovers to support the concert.

As it happened the Summer Concert was a great success. The headline in the Mercury declared that "LSO Concert Was Like Old Times" and the critic felt sure that crisis reactions to the war had not killed the love of music. The orchestra was on form in Weber's Oberon overture, Rossini-Respighi's La Boutique Fantasque and Valse Triste and Finlandia by Sibelius. Cyril Smith played the Brahms Second Piano Concerto and was such a success that he gave three encores.

The critic in the Mail noted that the khaki in the audience and the glorious show of tulips in the De Montfort Hall Gardens were contrasting features of a tremendously enjoyable concert. He reported "a big audience enjoying a couple of hours brilliant playing by the LSO and one of the outstanding English pianists of the day".

At the back of the printed programme for this concert, Arthur Thornley contributed an interesting article entitled "What Shall I Play?" It was really a plea for parents to encourage their children to take up instruments other than the violin. Apparently, the LSO had been "inundated" with requests from young violinists all wishing to play with the orchestra. The problem was that there was a full complement of violins as well as a long waiting list of hopefuls, whereas for other instruments the situation was quite different. Thornley makes an interesting point: "Full use cannot be made of potential talent in the orchestral field unless - for every child who takes up the violin, another takes up one of the lower strings (viola, cello or double bass) whilst another young musician devotes his attention to the wind section and yet another to the brass." He goes on to say "If, therefore, the next generation of Leicester music lovers is to hear orchestral music played by local musicians and the instrumental talent of our young people is to be used to best advantage, it is essential that beginners should be encouraged to explore the possibilities of the less familiar instruments".

Photo of Sargent and Karl Russell on the porch of Russell's house Ratcliffe Road, Stoneygate, Leicester, taken around 1940.

In an article in the Leicester Evening Mail Sargent's rehearsal style is discussed. The writer noted what a wonderful way he had of making everyone enjoy the music. But that wasn't surprising as he seemed to be enjoying it so much himself. He occasionally broke off to tell the players the story of the piece they were playing. One member of the orchestra, who had played under Sargent for twenty years considered him one of the finest and most able conductors in the world.

There was a real sense of pride amongst the players that despite his international fame and enormous workload, Sargent was still the conductor of the Leicester Symphony Orchestra. They felt honoured that someone who was now so well known should return season after season to take their concerts. For Sargent's part, he felt he owed the orchestra a great deal. It had given him many opportunities and enabled him to work with some of the finest musicians of the day. He had learned a considerable amount from his years with the LSO. It was a fruitful and happy relationship for both parties. However, the time was approaching when it really would be impossible for Sargent to continue as the orchestra's principal conductor. The war had increased the audience for orchestral music and Sargent was one of the most popular conductors working in England. Consequently he was in tremendous demand the length and breadth of the country.

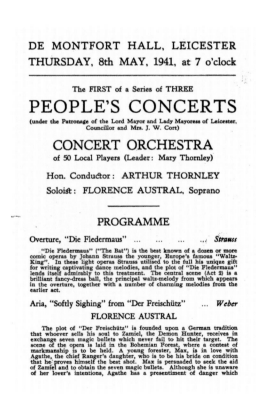

DE MONTFORT HALL, LEICESTER
THURSDAY, 8th MAY, 1941, at 7 o'clock

The FIRST of a Series of THREE

PEOPLE'S CONCERTS
(under the Patronage of the Lord Mayor and Lady Mayoress of Leicester, Councillor and Mrs. J. W. Cort)

CONCERT ORCHESTRA
of 50 Local Players (Leader: Mary Thornley)

Hon. Conductor: ARTHUR THORNLEY
Soloist: FLORENCE AUSTRAL, Soprano

PROGRAMME

Overture, "Die Fledermaus" ... ... *Strauss*

"Die Fledermaus" ("The Bat") is the best known of a dozen or more comic operas by Johann Strauss the younger, Europe's famous "Waltz-King". In these light operas Strauss utilised to the full his unique gift for writing captivating dance melodies, and the plot of "Die Fledermaus" lends itself admirably to this treatment. The central scene (Act 2) is a brilliant fancy-dress ball, the principal waltz-melody from which appears in the overture, together with a number of charming melodies from the earlier act.

Aria, "Softly Sighing" from "Der Freischütz" ... *Weber*

FLORENCE AUSTRAL

The plot of "Der Freischütz" is founded upon a German tradition that whoever sells his soul to Zamiel, the Demon Hunter, receives in exchange seven magic bullets which never fail to hit their target. The scene of the opera is laid in the Bohemian Forest, where a contest of marksmanship is to be held. A young forester, Max, is in love with Agathe, the chief Ranger's daughter, who is to be his bride on condition that he proves himself the best shot. Max is persuaded to seek the aid of Zamiel and to obtain the seven magic bullets. Although she is unaware of her lover's intentions, Agathe has a presentiment of danger which

Front cover of People's Concerts programme from May 1941.

So it was that barely a year after the war had begun, Sargent handed the baton over to Arthur Thornley with the instruction to keep the orchestra going as well is possible under the wartime conditions. Once again, Thornley stepped in to a difficult situation and managed to turn it into a remarkable success.

In his own words, Arthur Thornley "began cautiously with two series of popular concerts with a small orchestra of about twenty four players in the New Walk Art Gallery on Saturday afternoons". He then goes on to say, "But by the summer of 1941 we were back in the De Montfort Hall with a full orchestra under the title "The People's Concert Orchestra", reverting back to the name of Leicester Symphony Orchestra for the few concerts which Dr. Sargent and other guest conductors were able to direct."

This characteristically modest statement gives very little idea of Thornley's true achievement. Were it not for him, the orchestra would have ceased to exist. He worked tirelessly and thanks to his own musical and administrative talents amateur music flourished in Leicester in the dark days of the early forties.

In an article in the Leicester Evening Mail of 19 July 1940, headed "Keeping Music Alive" Suzanne Harrison states "No one has worked harder during the war to keep music alive than Mr. Arthur Thornley. He has had the support of many members of the Leicester Symphony Orchestra. Last night at the Little Theatre he provided us with a real feast of popular music, mostly from operas". The Leicester Mercury, under the heading "Versatile Musician" began an article on the same day with the statement that "Mr Arthur Thornley is generally acknowledged to be the most versatile musician in Leicester at the present time. Not only can he play about every instrument in the orchestra but he can orchestrate and conduct".

Ernest Gorham Gee, an influential and respected local musician, is quoted as describing Thornley as "the finest amateur musician in Leicester". The same article goes on to make reference to Thornley's habit of "slipping round here, there and everywhere, looking after the artists, taking his place in the orchestra or seeing after various business odds and ends that crop up during the evening. Yet he is always unruffled and unperturbed – at least, he seems so".

It is these qualities that made Thornley the man Sargent felt he could trust. His instinct proved right; as not only did Thornley keep things going, he also produced some very impressive performances if contemporary reviews are anything to go by. At a concert in the Edward Wood Hall the orchestra "shone brilliantly" and gave a "memorable" performance in the De Montfort Hall of Dvorak's New World Symphony later that year. The following season the orchestra programmed Beethoven's Fifth Symphony, known during wartime as the "Victory Symphony" due to the resemblance of its principal theme to the dots and dashes of the letter V in Morse code. The Leicester Evening Mail thought it a "workmanlike performance" but claimed that the orchestra under Thornley had "gained greatly in strength since it first so gallantly sought to keep Leicester supplied with music". The soloist at the concert was Benno Moiseiwitsch who played Grieg's Piano Concerto - proving that Thornley was able to attract leading musicians to wartime Leicester.

Sargent returned to the orchestra in December 1941 for a programme featuring Louis Kentner in Franck's Symphonic Variations and Liszt's E flat Piano Concerto. It was a lengthy programme as Smetana's Overture to the Bartered Bride, Tchaikovsky's Marche Slave and Borodin's Second Symphony were also played. The critics were pleased to see Sargent back, even though LS in the Evening Mail referred to him as Dr Malcolm Campbell! In the Leicester Mercury, Kentner was described as "a pianist of quite unusual gifts". This was followed by a revealing comment: "His control over tone goes hand in hand with a certain largeness of conception linked with a highly personal outlook. He is no easy performer to follow for his

THE ORCHESTRA

First Violins :
Mrs. Arthur Thornley
Mr. F. Mountney
Mr. Lewis Birkett
Mr. Leslie Mansfield
Miss Joyce Mountney
Mrs. K. M. Greer
Mrs. G. Foss
Mrs. E. Colledge
Miss A. W. Pooley
Miss J. Gedye
Mrs. S. Shield
Mr. J. Guyan

Second Violins :
Miss R. Tillyard
Miss Ethel Hicks
Miss M. Groocock
Mrs. R. P. Shea
Miss C. Kibart
Mr. R. Rudd
Mrs. P. W. Neale
Mrs. G. Cooper
Miss M. Bown
Miss M. Stafford
Mr. H. T. Woolston
Mrs. E. Wraight

Violas :
Mr. A. J. de Reyghère
Mr. P. W. Neale
Mrs. G. Sirrell
Mr. R. E. Getliffe

Violas—contd.
Mr. E. Busby
Mr. P. W. Richardson
Miss M. Goould
Miss M. S. Furness

Violoncellos :
Mrs. R. L. Robertson
Mr. C. H. Mansfield
Mr. A. Coleman
Mr. J. Coney
Mrs. M. S. Bryce
Mr. K. Holyoake
Miss B. Freer

Basses :
Mr. F. T. Dawson
Mr. E. J. Ward
Miss E. Revell
Mr. W. E. Freer

Flutes :
Mr. F. Dyson
Mr. C. W. Quarmby
Major R. P. Shea

Oboes :
Mr. I. Slaney
Mr. H. W. Tharp

Clarinets :
Mr. A. V. Palmer
Miss M. Collis

Bass Clarinet :
Mr. S. R. Kenworthy-Browne

Bassoons :
Mr. H. W. Bird
Miss E. M. Lloyd

Horns :
Mr. K. E. Winkless
Mr. F. W. Hyde
Mr. R. F. Wood
Mr. G. H. Baker

Trumpets :
Mr. S. S. H. Iliffe
Mr. E. C. Moore
Mr. R. Tillyard

Trombones :
Mr. D. G. Burditt
Mr. L. J. Tyers
Mr. A. Haseldine

Tuba :
Mr. A. E. Morris

Timpani :
Mr. L. G. Collis

Percussion :
Mr. G. F. Hardcastle
Mr. J. Sharp

Harp :
Miss P. Durston

LSO player list from the January 1942 concert programme. The reference to the Czech army choir and band reflects the fact that we are three years into World War II.

music has sometimes a sort of Narcissus interlude in which it pauses to gaze at itself appreciatively."

Help with sponsorship came from CEMA (Council for the Encouragement of Music and Arts) who had been impressed by Thornley's efforts to the extent that it supported three De Montfort Hall concerts. Karl Russell also revived his interest and promoted four Sunday concerts.

In December 1941 the death was announced of Ernest Gorham Gee. He had been a good friend to the orchestra for many years both as a committee member and as a generous benefactor who made it possible for the LSO to present world-renowned soloists. Gee was a member of a well known and influential local family. He had a profound love of music and was a notable pianist who composed a number of short works for the instrument. He was also one of the founders of the Leicester Competitive Music Festival and for twenty one years was its treasurer and chief organiser. He helped many young musicians both practically and financially and would entertain his own children on the piano each evening before they went to bed. He was a great friend of Malcolm Sargent who was often to be found as a guest at Gee's fine house at the top of Leicester's New Walk, where they would enjoy lively parties or musical evenings.

The year 1942 began with the renowned pianist Solomon appearing with Thornley and the orchestra in Beethoven's C minor Concerto. It was also at this concert that Thornley's own arrangement of Bach's Toccata and Fugue in D minor was heard for the first time. A few weeks later the young Ida Haendel played the Beethoven Violin Concerto in a testimonial concert for a local violinist Frank Muston, who was recovering from a long and serious illness. In May, leading British singers including Eva Turner and Roy Henderson came to take part in an operatic excerpts programme that included Thornley's arrangement of the Grand Chorus, March and Ballet Music from Verdi's Aida. The De Montfort Hall was packed for this event which was "enthusiastically enjoyed".

Later in the year on July 26, at a Sunday afternoon concert, the orchestra scored a huge success with a popular programme featuring Richard Addinsell's Warsaw Concerto, Gershwin's Rhapsody in Blue, Prokofiev's Peter and the Wolf (the first

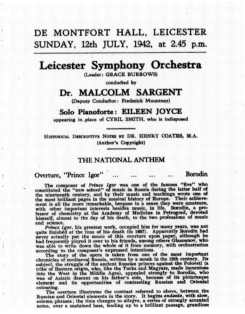

Front cover of concert programme 12 July 1942. Thought to be Sargent's last LSO concert.

performance in Leicester) and some well known vocal items from popular local singer and impresario Lillian Dunkley. The De Montfort Hall was packed and hundreds had to be turned away. The pianist was Irene Kohler and the narrator Irene Malin.

Clifford Curzon appeared at the November concert when he played a Mozart concerto and various solo items by Liszt. The orchestra played Humperdinck's Hansel and Gretel Overture, Grieg's Sigurd Jorsalfar Suite and Arthur Bliss's music from Things to Come. Leading soprano Gwen Catley sang items by Saint-Saens and Ambroise Thomas. This was another occasion when the size of the audience exceeded expectations, thus giving the organisers considerable cause for optimism.

In July 1943, Arthur Thornley took the orchestra (this time billed as the Leicester Symphony) to Luton as part of the town's "Holiday Entertainments". Two programmes were given. The first, in the afternoon, was billed as "Music for Youth" and included Quilter's Children's Overture and Prokofiev's Peter and the Wolf. Irene Kohler played the Grieg Piano Concerto. The critic was enthusiastic. The headline for the double review read "Two Good Concerts Open Luton Musical Season". He then describes the quality of the playing. The strings were "for the most part very good and the brass (especially the horns), excellent". The playing of the Grieg was "flawless". Later he goes on to say that despite some less distinguished woodwind playing, "the heart of this orchestra is truly sound".

The evening concert included the famous Luton Girls' Choir in a group of choral pieces. The orchestra played Bliss's Things to Come, the Swan Lake Suite and Thornley's own

> Unfortunately Dr. Sargent replied stating that owing to the fact that he will not have a free weekend between now and the end of next July, he considered it utterly impossible for him to accept the Conductorship pf the Orchestra, but suggested that the Leicester Symphony Orchestra remain in existence, doing smaller concerts, accompanying 'Messiahs' Etc. Dr. Sargent sincerely hoped that he would not be accused of 'Ratting' but made the splendid suggestion that the Conductorship remain open, and the choice of Guest Conductors for any important concerts be left to the discretion of the new Committee. Dr. Sargent conveyed his best wishes and earnest desire to be accouainted with events transpiring at the general meeting to be held on the 29th August 1943.
>
> In view of the decision of Dr. Sargent, the Committee considered it necessary for a Deputy Conductor to be nominated. Mr. F.Mountney, Mr. A.J. De Reyghere, and Mr. A.Thornley were approached on this matter, but both Mr. Mountney and Mr.Thornley prefer not to accept this Office, the latter frankly admitting that Mr. De Reyghere, who kindly consented to being nominated for this position, was best fitted for this Office. The question of rehearsals was discussed, but it was decided that this matter should be left until the general meeting, on the 29th August 1943, and be thrown open for discussion.

Extract of a minute dated August 22, 1943 from the official LSO records, where Sargent explains that it would be "utterly impossible" for him to conduct LSO - for at least the next eleven months. The second paragraph discusses who the replacement conductor should be.

transcription of Bach's D minor Toccata and Fugue (which the critic described as "workmanlike"). Irene Kohler was the soloist in Rhapsody in Blue and the Warsaw Concerto. She got a rave review for her versatile and stylish playing, but the orchestra was not on quite such good form as in the earlier concert. Nevertheless this double event was undoubtedly an overall success and a big boost to the orchestra's prestige.

However, back in Leicester things were rather less amenable. The war had caused a great demand for classical music and naturally enough, the professional orchestras took full advantage of the situation. This meant that by 1943 non-professional orchestras like the LSO began to find themselves almost squeezed out by the big names. In fact Sargent himself was one of the busiest conductors in England at this time and although he had withdrawn from the LSO, he was touring the country with the London orchestras and giving concerts in cinemas and any other venues large enough to house them. This had particular relevance to Leicester due to the quality of its hall.

Although it came close to destruction when a landmine dropped on the pavilion in nearby Victoria Park, the De Montfort Hall remained unscathed by the war. Consequently it was a popular port of call for visiting orchestras as it was undoubtedly the finest concert hall in the Midlands and one of the best in the country. It wasn't just classical music that was in demand; there were more dance band concerts and Sunday afternoon events. Arthur Thornley felt that local players, who had kept music alive during the first part of the war, were being sidelined in favour of big names and audiences for LSO concerts were suffering. Particularly annoying was a concert given by the Liverpool Philharmonic Orchestra which had recently appointed Sargent as its conductor. It took place just two days before an LSO concert. Needless to say the financial effects on the LSO were disastrous. Thornley was in fighting mood and took on the Parks Committee and the Corporation. His main complaint was that the Parks Committee had very little collective musical knowledge and was not helping the situation by booking all these visiting ensembles. There should be an advisory group set up consisting of "discriminating musicians" to ensure "high artistic aims". Whether he thought that he should be included in his proposed group he does not say, but it is quite clear that he felt very strongly about what was happening.

The plight of the LSO had reached the ears of William Glock, at that time one of the country's leading music critics, whose column in the Observer was read by virtually all discriminating musicians. Glock was later to become a visionary, if controversial, Controller of Music at the BBC. So intrigued was he that he came to Leicester on a two day visit in January, 1944. His mission was to see for himself just what was facing the local musicians and whether Thornley's complaints were justified. He produced a lengthy article in the following week's Observer in which he laid out the situation in the city (which he felt could apply to any similar city) and made reference to both the choral and orchestral tradition. He felt that before the war with Sargent at the helm of both the LSO and the Philharmonic Choir, Leicester's musical diet was "both ambitious and varied". But with the rise of a new type of concert-goer who "is prepared to go to anything that could be called entertainment; and the spectacle of a large orchestra with an agitated conductor and a well-known soloist falls into this category", things changed. "Meanwhile the seasoned Leicester audience is dying out and so an entirely new balance of interest was created, with young audiences flocking to hear the Grieg and Tchaikovsky concertos…and great choral works were ignored unless a fashionable conductor happened to beat his way through them."

There is no doubt that Glock had some sympathy with Thornley's views and made a number of suggestions. The first was to take the running of the De Montfort Hall away from the Parks Committee. Glock advised that the committee should be "non agricultural and should regulate all music at the De Montfort Hall so that the proper things are supported". Secondly he suggested that the local orchestra "should aim at distinctive programmes; i.e. it should provide music which commercial orchestras have no intention of risking. (These orchestras do much good in setting a standard of performance and much harm in fostering a one-sided outlook)". Finally he felt that there should be a first class professional orchestra created to serve the East Midlands.

Glock's comments drew a mixed response from local figures. The music critic in the Leicester Mercury, CAT, took a surprisingly forthright view. He stated that there was nothing wrong with giving dates to visiting orchestras and bands if they "fetch in the crowds" and that the policy "has brought Leicester more first-class playing than it has ever heard before and those who criticise it should accept the onus of showing how it could be done better".

He also dismissed the idea of a regional orchestra on the grounds that it would not have enough work to keep it in business. He felt that Thornley was unnecessarily pessimistic in his outlook and that the situation was only a temporary one. He finished his comments thus: "Meanwhile, though there are Jeremiahs a-jeremiahing most of us are doing very well, thank you. We are paying for a good article and seeing that we get it."

More controversy followed. Thornley responded by saying that he was not pessimistic and felt that given time Leicester could have as fine an orchestra as Liverpool if there was the financial backing to achieve it. CAT then countered: "We may take it then that Mr Thornley is prepared, with the assistance of his committee of experts, to shoulder the task of preparing for our future delectation a Leicester Symphony Orchestra of quality comparable with the Liverpool orchestra." He went on to say that he felt the LSO had "missed the bus" as at the beginning of the war it had a "first class conductor and a reputation forming a solid foundation on which to build".

This seems rather unfair to Thornley who was left holding the baby after Sargent's departure. With half his players mobilised, it is a wonder that he kept the orchestra going at all. Quite justifiably, Thornley (who did not really wish to continue the argument in the press) felt bound to reply to CAT's comments. They are worth quoting at length. He pointed out that the LSO was one of the first orchestras to resume its activities under wartime conditions and that after Sargent's resignation he had "endeavoured to fill the breach by conducting over fifty musical performances in two years". He goes on to say: "It would be idle to pretend that these performances would bear comparison with those now being given by all-professional visiting orchestras, but they held together the best of Leicester's orchestral players, attracted large and appreciative audiences whilst the standard of performance was generally commended by the distinguished soloists who worked with the orchestra."

Thornley then recalls that towards the end of 1942, "the volume of musical traffic passing through Leicester increased so much that it was impossible to run a local orchestral service without serious risk of clashing with musical "tourists" of all types and after two or three more costly trips the LSO's "utility" bus had to come off the road". He concludes by saying, "Under these circumstances CAT's references to "missing the bus" are a little irritating – particularly to me, having had to drive and conduct the only regular orchestral bus service in Leicester for two years. Room for a good local orchestra should be made not by cutting off the supply of first-class visiting orchestras but by eliminating some of the inferior stuff. I don't think that CAT would quarrel with this and I feel he is a little hasty in his surmises and premature with his criticism."

Here the correspondence ends, but it is impossible not to admire Thornley's robust defence of both himself and the LSO. He was, after all, a local businessman who made music as a hobby, yet the time and effort he devoted to the affairs of the Leicester Symphony Orchestra ensured its survival at a time when many other amateur musical organisations around the country were going under.

At one point in the controversy, the committee had recommended suspension of the orchestra's activities until circumstances proved more favourable but this was met with very strong opposition. There was an impasse and the officers and committee, including Thornley, resigned en bloc. A new committee was formed but that too encountered a number of constitutional as well as practical difficulties, but it did manage to appoint Karl Russell as the orchestra's new president, Alfred De Reyghere as deputy conductor and Robert Silvester as leader. Then, as Thornley recalled in 1972, "having done this, the new committee was forced to the same conclusions as the

PHOTO: COURTESY OF NEIL CRUTCHLEY

Robert Silvester, from a Leicester Choral & Dramatic Society programme of 1938. He joined LSO (first violins) in the 1920s and was leader in 1944. He also played in 1953 and 1954.

one it had replaced and appealed to me and several other former officers to resume the positions from which we had resigned".

The orchestra was soon back in its stride and the concert in May 1944, was conducted by Basil Cameron, a well-known figure of the day and stalwart of the London Promenade Concerts. He had two very distinguished piano soloists, Benjamin Britten and Clifford Curzon. Curzon gave a "vigorous" performance of Rachmaninov's Second Concerto and joined Britten in the composer's own Scottish Ballad for two pianos and orchestra. LS, in the Leicester Evening Mail thought it "a novelty" and described it as a "clever, modern, sometimes hilarious, always amusing parody". It was given a "brilliant" performance by both soloists and orchestra. However, he described the playing of the opening work, Weber's overture to Oberon as "rather grim".

The critic commented that he hoped the orchestra would be able to carry on "in spite of the many difficulties which present themselves at present". He thought the standard of playing had "never been so high as it is now" his comment on Oberon notwithstanding. Thornley said they were hoping to give two concerts in the Temple Speech Room in Rugby under Alfred de Reyghere who was the music master at Rugby School.

These concerts, held on the same day, were a sell-out and judged a great success with the critic of the Rugby Advertiser stating that, "The Midlands should take this orchestra to its heart". The popular programmes included works by Beethoven, Brahms, Elgar, Schubert, Addinsell and Tchaikovsky. By all accounts the orchestra was on good form and the reviewer concluded his comments by stating that, "It (the LSO) has shown great ability and much willingness to shoulder tremendous burdens and judging by the acclamation at these concerts, both Mr de Reyghere and the Leicester Symphony Orchestra can be assured of a warm welcome whenever another visit to Rugby can be planned".

The November concert saw Basil Cameron back on the LSO rostrum in a very popular programme that took no risks with the box office returns: Beethoven's Leonora Overture No.3 and Emperor Concerto and Dvorak's New World Symphony.

By the end of the war, Arthur Thornley was beginning to take a less prominent role in the dealings of the Leicester Symphony Orchestra in order to further his interest in the performance of opera with the Leicester Opera Club and the Leicester Operatic Players. He had almost unwittingly become the LSO's conductor, originally "holding the fort" for Sargent and then taking over when it became clear that the latter would not be able to continue due to his ever increasing national and international commitments. His successor as conductor of the orchestra was his deputy, Alfred de Reyghere, who had scored such a notable success in Rugby.

8. Post War Struggles

The immediate post-war period was a time of difficulty for the Leicester Symphony Orchestra. As with many other local bodies its funds were depleted and there were many changes in personnel both on the musical and the administrative fronts. However, the orchestra's new conductor, Alfred de Reyghere, was proving to be an impressive orchestral trainer who maintained a high standard of playing and discipline. He is remembered by one player as "very efficient, although rather impatient and bad tempered, but he got good results and was a fine musician". Another said, "Alfred was a very shrewd and perceptive musician. He didn't suffer fools gladly but he got good results with the material he had and very little escaped his notice".

Early in de Reyghere's tenure, the orchestra gave a number of special concerts for troops in military establishments. The programmes consisted mainly of popular classics interspersed with the odd rarity. In general these troop concerts were well received and were given in conjunction with the orchestra's regular appearances at the De Montfort Hall. In January 1946 pianist Benno Moiseiwitsch was the guest artist, which proves the orchestra was still capable of attracting big names. He played Beethoven's C minor Concerto and the rest of the programme consisted of Bach's Third Brandenburg Concerto, The Swan of Tuonela by Sibelius and Brahms' Second Symphony.

However, the financing of future concerts was giving cause for concern. The LSO had run down its reserves to a dangerous level over the war years and now the situation was becoming critical. One incident that did not help the orchestra's fortunes was a serious disagreement between the Hon Secretary (Mr Hampson) and Karl Russell, the cause of which seems obscure but resulted in Russell's resignation as president. This was quite a blow at a time when finances were at a low ebb. Russell was an excellent fundraiser and was also prepared to dip into his own pocket if occasion demanded. Fortunately, the exile did not last and Russell subsequently accepted the chairmanship of an organisation formed to raise funds and known as The Association of Friends of the Leicester Symphony Orchestra. Sargent agreed to be its president.

Karl Russell's successor as the orchestra's president was Dr Kenneth Greer. He held the post from 1945 to 1950 and succeeded in keeping the orchestra afloat during those troubled years. The orchestra's first president, Baroness Ravensdale, who had given tremendous support during the first two decades of the LSO's life, was made its patron.

The Association of Friends flourished and by the end of 1946 it had well over two hundred

COURTESY: LINDSAY WALLACE

LEICESTER SYMPHONY ORCHESTRA

Conductor : Alfred de Reyghére

MOURA LYMPANY

PIANOFORTE

in the

Temple Speech Room

(By kind permission of the Headmaster)

Wednesday July 18th

at 7 p.m.

PROGRAMME

Overture : Leonora No. 3	. . .	Beethoven
Piano Concerto in A Minor	. . . .	Grieg
Symphony No. 5 in C Minor	. .	Beethoven

TICKETS: 7/6 5/- 4/- (Unreserved) 3/-

Booking commences 2.30 p.m. Saturday July 7th at Hansons, Church Street

printed by the maple press ● rugby

This poster was found in a second-hand bookshop in Market Harborough and is from 1946. The logo at the top relates to Hospital Effort and bears the initials BTH and AA. Alfred de Reyghere joined LSO in February 1927 and was conductor during 1946.

members and associates. The subscription was a guinea (£1.05) for full membership and five shillings (25p) for associate membership. For this, subscribers could attend a monthly meeting with a guest speaker or performer. Between November 1946, and March 1947, these included Alfred de Reyghere talking about "The LSO and the next programme", a musical evening from Vera McNeill, a talk on "Woodwind with Instrumental Illustrations" from Arthur Thornley and a recital by the Haydn Hopkins Trio.

In the programme for the concert October 17, 1946, the Association of Friends placed a full page advertisement which began with this impressive statement, "Leicester has a symphony orchestra, and it is the object of the Association of Friends to give it all the backing and encouragement in its power. It is hoped that in the not too distant future the LSO will be accorded that civic recognition which other orchestras in the country enjoy, and which the people of a city of the size and importance of Leicester have a right to expect. Only can the LSO achieve this if it receives the moral and financial support of the people of Leicester. WILL YOU HELP?" The response was encouraging.

The orchestra managed to keep together despite its financial problems and produced some attractive programmes. For October 1946, Prokofiev's Classical Symphony rubbed shoulders with Benjamin Dale's English Dance and the distinguished French violinist, Jean Pougnet was the soloist in Mozart's D major Concerto. The headline in the Leicester Mercury stated "Leicester Symphony Orchestra Merited Bigger Audience" and began the review by noting the hall was "scarcely half full" and "the orchestra deserved better than this".

Pougnet played the Mozart concerto with "authority and brilliance and de Reyghere conducted "with a violinist's understanding". The concert ended with Beethoven's Eroica Symphony which was described as the "main proving ground of the evening". The conductor "missed some of the elegiac grandeur of the slow movement and more than one department dropped an occasional stitch, thereby maintaining a sense of adventure in the performance". This remark could be taken two ways but the reviewer, WHW, does go on to say that "the attack was vigorous and intelligent" and that "the essential Beethoven came through in the mighty climaxes".

The review ends with a delightful comment on the opening piece. "The orchestra's one departure from the classics, Dale's English Dance, was the one occasion when they were anything like at sea. Well, if not at sea, at least in the pier pavilion!"

An even smaller audience turned up in November to hear Denis Matthews play Beethoven's Piano Concerto No.4. Warwick Braithwaite was the guest conductor and the rest of the programme comprised Weber's Der Frieschutz Overture and Elgar's Enigma Variations.

Another guest conductor appeared in March 1947; Clarence Raybould, Sir Adrian Boult's assistant with the BBC Symphony Orchestra. His lengthy programme featured Wagner's Meistersinger Prelude, Handel's Water Music Suite, Mozart's Concerto for Two Pianos, Berlioz's

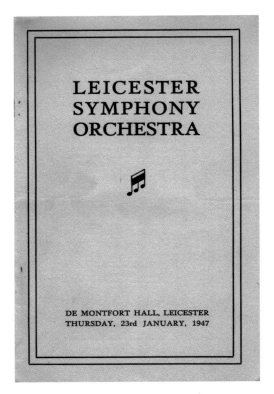

LEICESTER SYMPHONY ORCHESTRA

♫

DE MONTFORT HALL, LEICESTER
THURSDAY, 23rd JANUARY, 1947

Front cover of concert programme from January 1947.

Beatrice and Benedict Overture and Borodin's Symphony No.2.

Again there was a rather poignant comment in the Leicester Mercury about poor attendance, "the concert attracted an audience that must have disappointed the Leicester Symphony Orchestra, hardened though they surely are to such experiences. The gaps would have been worse but for the rows of school children". Those who stayed away missed "one of the most delightful experiences of the concert season in the playing of Ethel Bartlett and Rae Robertson in Mozart's Concerto for Two Pianos". The headline read "Nice Work on Two Pianos" and the reviewer, WHW, considered it an account in which "the subtle interplay of hand and thought added to the felicitous brilliance". The accompaniment was described as "quite pleasing".

The purely orchestral part of the concert received much less coverage but is worth quoting in full: "Clarence Raybould was the visiting conductor. He brought the best out of the orchestra in the climax of the Wagner and secured a neat performance of the Berlioz overture and a passable one of the Water Music. But the orchestra too often gave the impression of painstaking striving after adequacy. This they generally achieved – but they hadn't the little in hand that would have given the necessary abandon to Borodin's Second Symphony."

Financial problems were ever present, as there was less money from the wealthy benefactors who used to underwrite a large part of the orchestra's costs. Some had died and others simply did not have the resources they once had. However, the recently formed Association of Friends helped to fill the gap; but these were not easy years with, as Arthur Thornley remembers, "a disconcerting number of changes in the personnel of the executive officers and members of the committee".

As the decade drew to a close, concerts became less frequent and numbers attending dropped even more. But de Reyghere and the orchestra (now led by Blyth Major) kept going and produced some attractive programmes as one from January 1948 shows. It began with

Dvorak's rousing Carnival Overture and then George Eskdale was the soloist in Haydn's Trumpet Concerto. This was followed by the Theme and Variations from Tchaikovsky's Suite No.3 and the concert ended with Cesar Franck's Symphony in D minor.

There was what seemed to be the obligatory press comment about the "thin" audience which, in itself, must have been dispiriting to the players. On top of this, critical comment was very forthright during these years and WHW in the Leicester Mercury described de Reyghere's account of Franck's Symphony as "lacking certainty and articulation". It "had its moments but also its doldrums" and, in general "lacked the challenge which is essential to the work".

By the end of the 1940s, there was a realisation that the orchestra could no longer continue to give full scale symphony concerts in the De Montfort Hall. No one wanted the LSO to disband but things were about as bad as they could get. The determination of players and conductor to keep the orchestra going was as strong as ever, but there is no doubt that factors such as falling attendance, constant personnel changes, negative press criticism and row upon row of empty seats were beginning to affect morale. The war time surge in the popularity of classical music had subsided and even first class professional orchestras were not always able to fill the the De Montfort Hall's three thousand seats. The last year of the decade was the worst in the orchestra's history and financial and personnel problems meant that music making was becoming ever more difficult.

9. The 1950s -
Harry Shaw and Mary Thornley

At the turn of the decade the orchestra was on the verge of disbanding. In 1949 Alfred de Reyghere resigned as conductor and left the district. Blyth Major, who had also seen the orchestra through its worst times, was no longer the leader. No one seems to know the precise time of, or reason for, de Reyghere's departure. Even Arthur Thornley does not shed any light on the matter. He merely states that, "the minute book does not record why or when Alfred de Reyghere severed his active interest in the LSO". Perhaps he had become demoralised by the many problems the orchestra faced. He had served the LSO well for four seasons and given his services for no financial reward in order to keep the orchestra afloat. Whatever the reason, de Reyghere and Major both decided to sever their connections with the LSO at the same time. But it was not long before suitable replacements had been found. Harry Shaw was appointed as conductor and Mary Thornley was the new leader.

Harry Shaw was a professional baritone who had performed throughout England, often as a soloist for Malcolm Sargent. Shaw was a Lancastrian by birth and grew up in Blackburn. One of his friends was a fun loving young girl called Kathleen Ferrier. They went to the same singing teacher and later appeared as soloists on the same concert platform. Harry Shaw became a popular and much loved figure who enhanced the musical life of Leicester for more than forty years.

As a musician, Harry Shaw's talents were wide ranging. He was a fine pianist and organist, a superb choir trainer and one of Leicester's most distinguished teachers of music and singing. He was head of music at Wyggeston Girls School and his choir there was well known throughout the Midlands through their regular broadcasts on the BBC Midland Regional Service. He was also, at various times, organist and choirmaster of Victoria Road Church, St. James the Greater and St. Margaret's. However, it was as a clarinettist with the Army Pay Corps that his association with the LSO began. He was a recruit from the Pay Corps Band when it was stationed in Leicester during the latter part of the war. He stayed in the city after leaving the band and by the time the LSO needed a new conductor Shaw was a leading candidate. His period as conductor covered almost a decade, from the end of 1949 to to the end of 1958. In an article written in the Leicester Graphic in 1972, Arthur Thornley states that Harry Shaw "did much valuable work in re-establishing the orchestra and improving its standard under very difficult conditions".

Mary Thornley's connections with the LSO went back to the last concert of its first season, when at the age of fourteen she was invited by Sargent to join the violin section. She remained with the orchestra for seventy years and for almost half that time she was its leader.

A native of Leicester whose father was a professional musician, Mary Ashmell studied in Manchester with Arthur Catterall, a distinguished violinist of the day. She soon gained a reputation as a gifted player and a fine teacher. In 1933 she married Arthur Thornley, a local businessman and highly regarded amateur musician, who was at that time oboist and Honorary Secretary of the Leicester Symphony Orchestra. Both Arthur and Mary Thornley made an invaluable contribution to the life of the orchestra for a large part of the twentieth century. Mary also taught at Wyggeston Girls' School where she worked with Harry Shaw.

Due to the orchestra's precarious financial situation, the only practical step was to forsake the De Montfort Hall in favour of the Edward Wood Hall (now the Fraser Noble Hall) on London Road. Not only was this venue much less costly, it was also considerably smaller and could accommodate the loyal band of supporters without the endless rows of empty seats that were so disheartening in the larger hall.

Part of the financial problem, according to Arthur Thornley, was that although the Lord Mayor of Leicester had headed the LSO's list of patrons, and the Education Committee had made small grants towards rehearsal expenses, the orchestra had never received any practical help or encouragement in the thirty years since it was founded. This compared unfavourably with other cities where financial help was given on a regular basis. Thornley felt that even a modest grant of £500 a year would have enabled the orchestra to revert

Arthur Thornley in 1950. He joined LSO in the early years and was active as Chairman of LSO until 1977.

LSO leader Mary Thornley in 1950.

to giving four concerts each winter and to import outside professionals to strengthen its weaker departments. Also, it would have helped to recompense those who had seen the orchestra through its recent hard times. Like his predecessor, Harry Shaw conducted without a fee in order to conserve funds and to help pay for visiting soloists.

In June 1950, Shaw took a section of the orchestra to St Margaret's Church in Church Gate, Leicester, for a light concert with local baritone Malcolm Skillington as the guest soloist. This was a happy occasion as Shaw was the organist and choirmaster at St Margaret's and the proceeds from the concert went towards the church's organ fund; a very magnanimous gesture considering the orchestra's financial position. The programme included excerpts from Mendelssohn's Elijah, Grieg's Holberg Suite, two movements from Prokofiev's Classical Symphony, Elgar's Chanson de Matin and Massenet's Meditation from Thais with Mary Thornley as the violin soloist. The concert was judged a success and gave Harry Shaw a good opportunity to get to know the players on his home ground.

Within his first year as conductor, Shaw was producing attractive programmes with distinguished soloists. On April 3, 1951, he accompanied the great oboist Leon Goossens in concertos by Albinoni and Rutland Boughton. Mendelssohn's Italian Symphony, Bizet's second L'Arlesienne suite and Barber's Adagio for Strings were also played. Kathleen Long was the soloist in Mozart's A major concerto K488 in the following season and at the same concert, Beethoven's Eroica Symphony, Elgar's Serenade and Sibelius's Romance followed the Marriage of Figaro Overture.

Another big name to appear with the LSO at this time was the popular radio pianist Semprini, who was heard in the Grieg Concerto and a group of solos by Chopin and Liszt.

During these seasons, many works for string orchestra were featured. Harry Shaw and Mary Thornley both felt the confidence of the string section would improve by more exposure. Some of the pieces chosen, such as Barber's Adagio and the Romance by

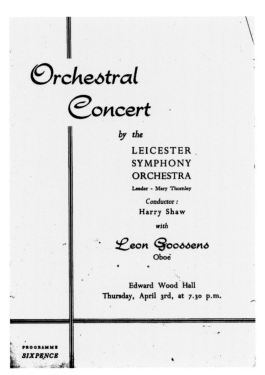

Cover of concert programme from April 1951. Note the concert venue, Edward Wood Hall – now Fraser Noble Hall.

Sibelius were unfamiliar to most of the players and were by no means easy to bring off. Consequently there were occasional "sticky moments" during performance, but overall the policy seemed to work and playing showed a small improvement. Newspaper reviews were fewer and shorter at this time but the general opinion was favourable and Shaw's liking for combining popular classics with less well-known works appeared to work well. For example, in October 1952, Alan Loveday was the soloist in Beethoven's Violin Concerto which followed the same composer's Egmont Overture, but in the second half Bizet's Symphony in C was played alongside the Irmelin Prelude by Delius and Britten's Soirees Musicales.

Another imaginative idea from February 1953 saw four of the orchestra's leading players acting as soloists. Cicely Kibart played the first movement of Saint-Saens' B minor Violin Concerto; Clifford Mansfield was heard in the first movement of the Lalo Cello Concerto, Arthur Field gave the Allegro from Weber's F minor Clarinet Concerto and Mary Thornley played part of Mozart's A major Violin Concerto. The orchestra's main contribution was Bizet's Symphony in C. This was repeated from the previous concert as due to a power failure, only one movement was performed on that occasion. This event drew a glowing report from the critic of the Leicester Mercury: "This was the most successful concert for a long time. Under Harry Shaw, the members displayed a newly found confidence giving precision of attack and better tone. There was also a much improved sense of rhythm. All the soloists did well."

The acclaim did not last for long however. In December of the same year, and back in the De Montfort Hall, the orchestra was accused of "playing below its best" even though the sound was much better after two seasons in the "doubtful" acoustics of the Edward Wood Hall. The reviewer continues: "Harry Shaw's conducting still does not give that light springing tempo we long to hear". Rossini's Barber of Seville Overture was described as "leaden footed" and although the "brilliant South African Pianist" Aronowitz, was praised for his performance of Liszt's First Piano Concerto, no mention at all was made of the main work of the evening, Dvorak's G major Symphony.

The inconsistency in the standard of playing was noticed by some of those in the audience at that time. One regular concert goer remembers the orchestra giving an extremely fine performance of Ravel's Pavane, yet "almost falling apart" in Tchaikovsky's Fourth Symphony. Another remembers the conductor's marvellous way with English music and his feeling for orchestral colour, but observed that on a number of occasions the orchestra was just not quite able to meet his demands.

Whatever their technical abilities, the members of the orchestra enjoyed performing with Harry Shaw. They respected his musicianship and his self-effacing attitude to his task. They also enjoyed some of the new works he introduced. One player remembers his patience and understanding when new pieces did not go as well as he had hoped. Generally, Shaw was a wise and sensitive conductor who never pushed his players beyond their capabilities but never accepted less than their best. He was also more than willing to hand over the baton to others and sometimes appeared as the vocal soloist.

One of the most enjoyable of these occasions was in March 1956, when the popular television personality and presenter of "Music for You", Eric Robinson, came to conduct and Harry Shaw sang arias from Tannhauser, Don Giovanni and Don Carlo. The orchestra, which by all accounts played well for its guest conductor, was heard in the Swan Lake suite, Eine Kleine Nachtmusick, The Antrim Hills and The Fair Day from Hamilton Harty's Irish Symphony and Bizet's second L'Arlesienne Suite.

Although critical reviews were infrequent and brief, the impression given is that the orchestra was keeping up a reasonable standard but with room for improvement. For example a comment from Ralph Pugsley in the Leicester Mercury in December 1955, states that the "Leicester Symphony Orchestra's playing showed that they are maintaining their standard without, perhaps, adding much". Harry Shaw was given credit for his interpretations of English and French works. A performance of Delius's Irmelin Prelude from around this time was described as "nicely played and interpreted" and Bizet's Jeux d'Enfants suite had "a delightful spring in its step with the conductor showing a natural feel for the lively Gallic style".

In December 1956, the internationally-known comedian and musician, Vic Oliver conducted the orchestra in a selection of popular pieces that included Khachaturian's Masquerade Waltz; Schubert's Unfinished Symphony and the ballet music from Gounod's Faust. Soprano Margaret Asher, a popular and significant local musician was the soloist on this occasion. She performed arias from La Traviata, Tosca and Rigoletto as well as Mozart's Alleluia from Exsultate Jubilate.

Vic Oliver was an interesting character. He was both a fast-talking, quick-witted comedian and a classically trained, serious musician. In the 1940s and 50s he was tremendously popular due to his regular appearances on the radio. He was a member

Cover of concert programme from December 1956, autographed by Vic Oliver.

of the team of the popular radio show "Hi Gang", which also featured Ben Lyon and Bebe Daniels. Oliver, who was born in Austria, fled the Nazis and went to America, where he established a name for himself both as a comedian and a musician. He then came to England where he was an instant success. Part of his comedy act was to play the violin – badly. But he was, in fact, an accomplished player who had studied at the Vienna Conservatoire in the 1920s, where his teachers included the great Moritz Rosenthal. He attended concerts given by the Vienna Philharmonic and, as a student, played in the Opera Orchestra under such great names as Bruno Walter and Otto Klemperer. Later he became the assistant conductor of the permanent opera at Graz. In 1945, along with his appearances as a comedian, Vic Oliver became the musical director of the British Concert Orchestra; a group that gave over a hundred concerts a year.

When Vic Oliver first appeared with the Leicester Symphony Orchestra, the programme contained an appreciation by the well-known music writer Hubert Foss which included these words: "As a musician, Oliver comes from a splendid training ground – the Vienna Conservatoire... As a comedian he brings to serious music an auxiliary adjunct by no means to be despised – the enviable power to attract an audience by his name and fame. I for one do not underrate the value of that as an inducement to musical appreciation.... Experience, skill, knowledge, a wide (and double) fame, and enduring love for the art – these are some of the qualities which Vic Oliver brings and offers to music today. He can do much for music and to his desire and power to do so, I give my wholehearted support."

Vic Oliver, who married Winston Churchill's daughter Sarah, conducted the LSO on three occasions; giving his services free of charge and attracting large audiences. He made a considerable contribution to the survival of the orchestra in difficult times.

The fact that guests of the calibre of Eric Robinson and Vic Oliver were prepared to conduct the LSO in the 1950s says something for the standard Harry Shaw maintained. After all, both the above artists were at the height of their popularity at this time and would not have lent their names to anything that was likely to reflect badly on them. Moreover, Vic Oliver is on record as describing Harry Shaw's LSO as "one of the best orchestras of its type in the country". He was also happy to become the orchestra's vice president, a post he retained until his death in 1962.

One former player remembered Oliver as "a remarkable musician, who really knew his stuff and tolerated no second rate playing". Another said, "We were lucky to have him and I suspect Arthur Thornley was somehow behind it. But whatever the case Oliver, the great comedian, took his music very seriously and when he was on the podium, he expected everyone else to do the same."

Not surprisingly, a musician of Harry Shaw's background had many personal friends in the world of professional music. Amongst their number was the internationally celebrated bass, Owen Brannigan. He appeared with the orchestra in November 1957 and sang a group of arias

LSO in November 1957. Owen Brannigan is the soloist with Harry Shaw on the rostrum. This is the only photo of Harry Shaw in the LSO archive.

and a collection of traditional folk songs. Included in the orchestral items were The Walk to the Paradise Garden by Delius and Beethoven's First Symphony. Due to Brannigan's huge popularity at the time, this concert drew a large and enthusiastic audience.

As the decade wore on the orchestra's programmes became less adventurous. Finances were precarious, and works like Schubert's Unfinished Symphony, Dvorak's New World Symphony and Grieg's Peer Gynt suites became staple fare. But Vic Oliver was still appearing with the LSO as late as May 1958, when amongst other things, he conducted Delius's On Hearing the First Cuckoo in Spring, Franck's Symphonic Variations (with Sheila Mossman on piano) and Bizet's two Carmen suites.

Occasionally the orchestra strayed from the De Montfort Hall. It played in the Town Hall, Burton upon Trent, in March 1956, when the renowned baritone John Cameron was the guest artist. He sang a selection of operatic arias and popular ballads and the orchestra played Mozart's Eine Kleine Nachtmusik, the March from Suite Algerienne by Saint-Saens and Delius's tone poem On Hearing the First Cuckoo in Spring. In Harry Shaw's last season the LSO appeared at Loughborough's Town Hall on two occasions. In the first concert Myra Mesaritis played the Grieg Piano Concerto and the orchestral items included La Boutique Fantasque and Bizet's first

The Orchestra

1ST VIOLINS
Mary Thornley (Leader)
Cicely Kibart
Christine Greer
Joyce Mounteney
Stella Shield
Walter Davis
Gilbert Holmes
Maud Bown
Reginald Rudd
Lilian Pooley
Doreen Adnet
Michael Fritche

12 *6*

2ND VIOLINS
Leslie Mansfield
Madge Stafford
Gertrude Cooper
Peter Mayes
Aileen Shelton
Christiana Wagstaffe
Irene Macmillan
R. Lonsdale
John Adnet
Irene Roberts
George Abrahams
Lilian Pollard

12 *6*

VIOLAS
A. H. Bass
Ernest Busby
Molly Gooud
Mary Folwell
Norman Perkins
Muriel Clague

6 *3*

CELLOS
Clifford Mansfield
Malcolm Fletcher
Allen Bosworth
Florence Bryce
Arthur Hunter
J. Adams
Shirley Halford
Dominic J. Sire
Avril Thackray

9 *4*

DOUBLE BASSES
M. Welford
H. W. Howard
A. B. Wiltshire
Edna Lake
E. Tansley

5 *3*

FLUTES
Charles Quarmby
Ernest Smith *2*

PICCOLO
Brian Johnson

OBOES
Terence Greer
Harry Tharp
W. L. Surman *2*

CLARINETS
Arthur Field
N. G. Pollard *2*

BASSOONS
Donald Gimson
Jill Sawbridge
J. Heal *2*

HORNS
Leonard Hartopp
Kenneth Winkless
Betty Anderson *2*

TRUMPETS
S. Iliffe
Kenneth Garner
Roland Johnson
J. Wyness *2*

TROMBONES
J. T. Stiles
T. B. Lee *2*

BASS TROMBONE
C. Hutt

TUBA
Albert Morris

TIMPANI
Phyllis De Mond *1*

PERCUSSION
J. Grainger

HARP
Olga Thornley

Joint Hon. Secretaries :
Miss C. Kibart, 20 Dumbleton Avenue, Leicester.
Mr. E. D. Smith, 165 South Knighton Road, Leicester.
Hon. Treasurer : Mr. N. C. Perkins, 36 Romway Road, Leicester.
L.P. Ltd.

LSO player list from November 1957.

L'Arlesienne suite. Later in the year, Suzanne Rosza from Hungary was the violin soloist. She played a Mozart Concerto and the Havanaise by Saint Saens. The other works included Schumann's First Symphony and Jeux d'Enfants by Bizet. One listener, who was present at both concerts, remembers the orchestra turning out impressive performances, with playing of a consistently good standard.

Vic Oliver with five violinists of LSO in 1958, with Mary Thornley on the left.

Towards the end of 1958, Harry Shaw's health began to give cause for concern and it soon became obvious that he would have to withdraw from the orchestra's 1959 season. Happily he made a good recovery but felt the time had come to relinquish the baton of the LSO and concentrate on his many other musical activities. He had seen the orchestra through some of its most difficult times and without his tenacity and professionalism, Arthur Thornley's determination and Vic Oliver's generosity, there would not have been an LSO by the 1960s.

Looking back over the decade's programmes, they reflect the conductor's wide-ranging tastes. As already shown, there was a good sprinkling of classics, but also many attractive smaller items that would have been less familiar to 1950s audiences. English and French music, especially works by Bizet, Ravel and Delius made regular appearances in his programmes and despite the generally small audiences, this was by no means a time of stagnation for the orchestra.

The search to find a successor to Harry Shaw had begun. There was one very obvious candidate and that was the orchestra's distinguished and long serving principal trumpet, Simeon Iliffe. He had been asked to deputise during Shaw's illness and had met with great success. However, he was already in his seventies and was looking towards retirement rather than new challenges.

10. Simeon Iliffe

There is no doubt that Simeon Iliffe was the right man for the Leicester Symphony Orchestra. What it needed more than anything else at this point in its life was a period of stability, and it was felt that Iliffe, with his vast experience and knowledge, was just the man to provide it. The years since the Second World War had not been easy as we have seen and by 1958 the fortunes of the LSO were once again at very low ebb. Harry Shaw's serious illness left the players without a conductor and swift action was needed.

It was agreed to ask Simeon Iliffe to stand in for Harry Shaw on a temporary basis. Iliffe had a reputation as an effective and experienced conductor in the brass band world, but he also had a reputation as a self effacing, modest man who disliked the limelight. Fortunately Iliffe agreed – albeit reluctantly, to give it a try. From the start it was clear that the right choice had been made, as Iliffe impressed both orchestra and audience with his excellent musicianship, personal charm and faultless and unruffled conducting style. He gave the orchestra confidence and a sense of security.

Simeon Sullivan Handel Iliffe was born in Fleckney, Leicestershire in 1889. His father and five brothers were all musicians. By the age of seven he "had the right mouth structure and teeth formation to tackle the cornet". His progress was swift and by his middle teenage years he was regarded as one of the county's leading players. His conducting career began at the remarkably young age of eighteen when he was appointed to the Leicester Imperial Band. This was an extraordinary achievement and a mark of the ability of someone who was not "pushy". As Iliffe himself recalled, "I learned my trade the hard way as there were no grants etc. available in those days".

He stayed with the Imperial Band guiding it through almost a hundred broadcasts as well as countless live performances. This was combined with his work as a gas fitter (he was district foreman at the Leicester Belgrave gas depot and retired in 1953 after 51 years service). Iliffe also conducted bands in Kibworth, Fleckney, Melton and Snibston. Add to this his numerous appearances as a trumpet and cornet player with many Midland and national orchestras and we get some idea of the wealth of knowledge and experience he brought to the LSO rostrum in 1959.

Simeon Iliffe may have been self taught as a conductor, but this did not mean that he was in any way deficient. His years with the bands had taught him the importance (particularly with amateurs) of a clear beat and plenty of cues. Anyone witnessing Iliffe on the rostrum would concede that he was a model of good, clear direction. He said conducting came naturally to him and that important attributes were a good sense of humour and lots of patience allied to firm control. Those who played for him all speak of his personal charm and kindness, his unfailing courtesy and good manners, excellent musicianship and endearing modesty. He insisted on high standards of playing and was not beyond making changes in personnel if he felt it necessary. Iliffe was considered to be one of Leicester's most distinguished musicians and like his predecessor, he was regarded as a friend by all who worked with him.

It is worth remembering that by 1959 Iliffe was already 70 years old. He had recently retired from the brass band world "to give a younger musician a chance" - an entirely characteristic gesture and one which had a bearing on his reluctance to accept any offer to conduct the LSO. However he could not stand by and watch the orchestra he had joined as a relatively young man almost forty years before, struggling for survival, so he "stood in" on the understanding that Harry Shaw would continue as conductor when he was well enough.

By the beginning of 1959 it was clear that Harry Shaw would have to reduce his workload and he resigned the conductorship of the orchestra. To the players and the committee the choice of his successor was obvious, but Simeon Iliffe was still reluctant to accept. However, Arthur Thornley used "every ruse in his repertoire" to persuade him and finally, he succeeded.

Iliffe's first concert, on April 7, consisted of Beethoven's Egmont Overture, Rachmaninov's Second Piano Concerto with Sidney Harrison as soloist, Arthur Thornley's transcription of Bach's Toccata and Fugue in D minor and Dvorak's Eighth Symphony. Ralph Pugsley, RAP of the Leicester Mercury, commented, "Mr Iliffe coaxed some good playing, particularly in the quiet passages but the louder moments had a tendency to become coarse and vulgar."

By the first concert of the following season, which took place on the November 24, it was clear that great strides had been made as Pugsley had this to say: "A deal of tidying up has been done since the Leicester Symphony Orchestra made its last public appearance. The conductor was Mr Simeon Iliffe and it was apparent that, in a few months, he has shaped his forces from what was previously a rather straggling and indecisive assembly of instrumentalists into something approaching a unified instrument with a sense of purpose and an increasing pride in precise performance". The music he had heard included Beethoven's Piano Concerto No. 3 with Phyllis Sellick and Symphony No. 2 in D major by Brahms.

Later in the season Iliffe took the orchestra to play in the Town Hall in Burton upon Trent where they were enthusiastically received. The programme included Schubert's Rosamunde Overture, Beethoven's Fifth Piano Concerto and another performance of Brahms' Second Symphony.

Under Iliffe's gentle but firm guidance the standard soon began to improve. His lifetime of experience was proving invaluable in orchestral training. One regular concert goer remembers a significant difference in the space of one season and by 1962 a transformation; fuller tone, more confidence, better attack and discipline and more excitement and expression in the interpretation of the music. Ralph Pugsley was also encouraging. He described Iliffe's account of Brahms' First Symphony given in April 1962 as "an intellectual's performance … ideally tough and taut and without mannerisms". He also thought the performance of Rossini's Semiramide Overture given at the same concert was "beautifully judged". The playing of the strings was "exceptionally fine … their sound rich and sensuous".

By November 1962, Pugsley's review was headed, "Leicester Symphony Orchestra At Their Post-War Best" and goes on to describe the concert as "a pleasurable occasion". He singled out Iliffe's account of Tchaikovsky's Fourth Symphony, saying that he had "imbued his players with a spirit of purposeful self-confidence which reflected unmistakably in their playing. The first and second violins produced tone of fine, glowing quality". He went on to praise the woodwind but suggested a few more cellos and basses would have made the string section even more impressive. However, there is no doubting his delight in what was, by any standards, a real step forward.

This improvement in the orchestra's musical fortunes was encouraging to the committee, but its members were concerned that there was not an equivalent improvement in box office returns. Concerts were still poorly attended with the gallery of the De Montfort Hall remaining closed. However these things tend to take time and, as the orchestra's reputation improved, so did audience numbers. The word got around.

In 1963, Philip Lank, the Leicester born Director of Music at Grantham Parish Church, invited the orchestra to Grantham to take part in a celebration concert to mark the

Leicester Symphony Orchestra At Their Post-War Best

Orchestra: Leicester Symphony. Conductor: Simeon Iliffe. Soloist: Ian Lake, piano.
Programme: Academic Festival Overture by Brahms; "La Source" ballet suite by Delibes; Rachmaninoff's second piano concerto; Symphony No. 4 by Tchaikovsky.

A PLEASURABLE OCCASION at Leicester De Montfort Hall, last night, because for me, this was the best post-war performance by the Leicester Symphony.

Their finest effort, unquestionably, was the Tchaikovsky fourth in which, from start to finish, there was proof that this ensemble of local musicians has now been welded into an orchestra—an instrument with a positive individuality instead of an erstwhile reputation for trying hard.

There is still room for improvement, but the future can be viewed optimistically by performer and listener alike for reason of the fact that there is now much to build upon.

Self Confident

Great credit is due to Mr. Iliffe who patently has done a worthwhile job of training and who also seems to have imbued his musicians with a spirit of purposeful self-confidence which reflected unmistakably in their playing.

The first and second violins produced tone of fine, glowing quality and their corporate feeling for a phrase will be improved upon even more when there is complete unanimity in bowing.

The violas were sound, but it needs a strengthening of the cello department and a couple more basses to eliminate obvious deficiencies in the string section as a whole.

Woodwind combined to present a well-balanced rich tone; horns were adequate, and the brass, solid in attack and precise as a whiprack, set a fine, brilliant edge on the climaxes.

It would be possible to indicate where, from a point of view of interpretation, more might have been done with certain passages. But that would be unfair to a conductor who, having brought his orchestra so far, is the best to know when his clear and definite beat can yield to the type of flowing line or impassioned gesture that evokes extreme delicacy or intense feeling.

As things are, Leicester Symphony's next concert can be looked forward to with pleasurable expectancy.

Variety Of Touch

An historic cycle was turned. I believe, when Leicestershire's Ian Lake played in the concerto. It was about 30 years ago when Sir Adrian Boult conducted the same work in Leicester with another local musician at the piano—Malcolm Sargent as he was at that time.

Ian Lake confirmed the good impression he made earlier in the year by his fine playing in the concerto and also his excellent performance of Rachmaninoff's preludes in E flat and G major and the famous "Polichinelle."

Mr. Lake brings a great variety of touch to his playing and he has the gift of projecting the listener forward. And that, of course, is the main secret of good performance.—R.A.P.

Leicester Mercury review of November 1962 concert.

church's five hundredth anniversary. The work was Handel's Messiah with the combined choirs of Grantham and the surrounding district. Lank conducted and the contralto soloist was another young Leicester artist who was destined for great things, Elizabeth Holden. In fact, two months later she appeared with the orchestra in the De Montfort Hall and gave a performance of Elgar's Sea Pictures which Ralph Pugsley described as "finely controlled, sensitively attuned to the atmosphere of each song and possessing moments of real beauty". He also enjoyed Iliffe's account of Mozart's Magic Flute Overture at the same concert which was "played with amazing sparkle". He said of conductor and orchestra, "the knack of doing musically the right thing came naturally".

Iliffe was not over-possessive about the orchestra and did not object to other conductors taking charge from time to time. Consequently the LSO was involved in such occasions as the Leicestershire and Rutland Federation of Women's Institutes and Townswomen's Guilds Jubilee Concert in 1965 when the conductor was the popular musical personality Stanford Robinson, and The City Schools Christmas Carol Concerts, which were always conducted by Dr D G Davies, the Advisor in Music to the City of Leicester Education Committee. The orchestra (much reduced in numbers) was frequently in the pit at the Little Theatre where it provided the accompaniment to many an amateur operatic production; sometimes Iliffe would conduct and on other occasions he would hand the baton to Arthur Thornley.

In the early sixties the LSO was involved in a film promoting Leicester's industrial, civic, cultural, sporting and educational life. City of Contrasts was produced by Edward Harris and directed by Steve Knight. Little seems to be known about the film, but one leading local historian thought that it was created as a project by students at the Teacher Training College at Scraptoft, in Leicestershire. There is a commentary by Martin Caven and the film features sections on the city's parks, housing, factories, civic life, Lord Mayor's procession, museums, schools, evening institutes and of course, the famous market. It is a fascinating document of a city that has changed a great deal since the film was made. At various times in its forty minute duration there is background music, and as the opening credits state, it is played by the Leicester Symphony Orchestra. The items comprised excerpts from Suppe's Poet and Peasant Overture, Beethoven's Pastoral Symphony, Weber's Invitation to the Dance, Paganini's Perpetuum Mobile and Straus's Tritsch Tratsch Polka. The standard of playing is astounding, even when taking into account the fact that a section of the film appears to be running at a faster speed than the rest, as people are walking as if in a silent film, and the music, at this point, Strauss's lively polka, sounds as if it is played at break-neck speed by a super-human virtuoso orchestra! But overall the soundtrack shows the LSO to be an impressive body, justifying the favourable comments of the time. The recording was made in 1963 in the upstairs room of Alderman Newton School where the LSO held their regular Sunday rehearsals.

PHOTO: COURTESY OF ROBERT KNIGHT

Massed school choirs in the mid 1960s. Note the now absent De Montfort Hall clock, top centre.

At one point in the film, a group of people are wandering around Leicester's New Walk Museum, and when they leave, they spot a poster announcing a concert by the LSO under Iliffe to take place on April 19. As they look approvingly at the poster, the scene changes to a shot of the exterior of the De Montfort Hall and then, just for a second, there's a very brief appearance of Simeon Iliffe in full evening dress, raising his baton.

In 2012, another film about Leicester, created by MACE and the University of Lincoln and entitled Made in Leicester, presented and narrated by Rosemary Conley and researched, written and produced by Radica Wright, used some excerpts from City of Contrasts and in these the LSO's impressive early 1960s playing can be heard again.

During the sixties the orchestra maintained a generally good standard, although the repertoire was fairly limited. There was far less French and English music than there had been under Harry Shaw and a greater emphasis on standard works to ensure as large an audience as possible. Symphonies by Beethoven, Brahms, Dvorak (the last three) Sibelius (one and two) and Tchaikovsky (also the last three) provided the backbone of the second part of each concert and there was always a popular concerto (Rachmaninov's Second, Tchaikovsky's First, Grieg or Schumann for piano, or the Brahms, Tchaikovsky, Mendelssohn, Bruch or Sibelius for violin).

Simeon Iliffe in 1968. He joined LSO in 1922 and appeared until May 1972. He was conductor from 1959.

Occasionally there were excursions into multiple soloists with the Brahms Double or the Beethoven Triple Concerto.

Iliffe's style on the rostrum was reassuring. His was a placid presence that never appeared to panic, even when things went awry, as on the odd occasion they did. His interpretations were well considered and weighty. He invariably adopted a sensible speed that allowed his players to phrase comfortably and gave the music time to breathe. There were those who felt that by the seventies, his performances lacked fire and excitement, but as was apparent at the Golden Jubilee concert in 1972, he was still capable of inspiring his players to a degree that would have been a credit to a conductor half his age.

By 1965 the orchestra was attracting its highest post war audiences and RAP finishes his review of the January 1966 concert by stating that the orchestra's "emergence from early post-war depression is one of the most encouraging and most influential things in Leicester's musical life". In November of that year, the orchestra gave the first performance in Leicester of Mahler's First Symphony which was well received and played with "really potent effect" despite a few shaky moments. Pugsley observed that "Simeon Iliffe radiated strength through calmness and his grasp of affairs was always unflinching. His cues were generous and one felt him to have devised a special stick technique for Mahlerian sub-division of beats". What more could an amateur orchestra ask of its conductor?

Many internationally known soloists appeared with the orchestra throughout the Iliffe years. These included Bronislav Gimpel, Alfredo Campoli, Alan Loveday, Louis Kentner, Denis Matthews, Barry Tuckwell, Leon Goossens, Amaryllis Fleming, Ian Wallace, Peter Katin, Jack Brymer, Stephen Bishop (now Kovacevick) and Shura Cherkassky. This illustrious list could serve as a comment on the fees charged by present day soloists, as it is unlikely that such celebrated names would be within the orchestra's budget in the twenty first century.

One particular concert in November 1967 featured both Amaryllis Fleming and the Alan Civil Horn Quartet. Fleming played the Haydn D major Cello Concerto and Civil's quartet gave what in 1967 was an extremely rare performance of Schumann's Concertstuck for Four Horns. Arthur Thornley was particularly pleased with this concert as not only was the orchestra performing two concertante works with well known soloists, the performance of the Schumann was thought to be the first in Leicester and it attracted people from all over the country.

An amusing incident is related concerning Louis Kentner's appearance as the soloist in Brahms' Piano Concerto No. 2 and it illustrates Iliffe's no-nonsense approach to his task. Kentner complained to the conductor that his piano stool was rather too high. Iliffe acted "swiftly and decisively" by borrowing a saw from one of the hall's handymen and cutting an inch off the legs of the stool.

At long last, Arthur Thornley's persistence paid off in another field, albeit rather modestly. In 1963 after years of lobbying, the orchestra was offered a grant of £500 a year from the General Purposes Committee. This had increased by the Golden Jubilee season in 1972 to £750. These grants, together with an annual £250 guarantee against loss from the National Federation of Music Societies, enabled the orchestra to operate for a number of years without undue financial anxiety. This was immediately noticeable in the improvement in the printed programmes which, for the first time for many years, contained analytical notes.

Early in 1967, the orchestra's committee asked Arthur Thornley to draft a new set of rules. These included "some clauses which may appear unnecessary or even objectionable at first sight", but Thornley explained the committee's reasons for their inclusion in a letter to players dated September 27. The clauses give some idea of the concerns of the orchestra at that time and as always, Thornley had the LSO's wellbeing at heart. One of the problems was to do with subscriptions:

"Rule 7 may create objections from a few members who for reasons which seem good to them have not paid a members' subscription for many years. Discussion on this matter at the last meeting of the committee revealed that there is strong

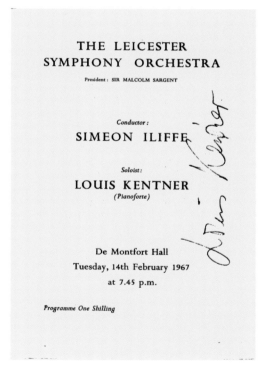

Cover of concert programme from February 1967, autographed by pianist Louis Kentner.

feeling amongst members that all who consider themselves to be permanent members of the orchestra and expect to participate in its concerts, should pay a subscription, and that it is unfair to others that some should be allowed "to get away without paying".

The problem of unpaid subscriptions was one that dogged the LSO in the 1960s and could have wider repercussions as Thornley went on to explain:

"Both the Leicester Corporation and the Arts Council attach great importance to evidence that playing members are bearing some of the share of the cost of running the orchestra, and the discrepancy between the number of regular members and total amounts of subscriptions has raised questions and comment. As this may prejudice further grants I hope that those who have not paid subscriptions in the past will not allow any personal feelings to jeopardise the financial security of the orchestra, which is mainly dependent on these grants."

Thornley then addresses another cause for concern:

"I have been specifically asked to include some rule to control the intrusion of odd people who, have turned up to play at rehearsals and concerts without the knowledge or consent of the conductor or hon secretary. Mr Iliffe has naturally been reluctant to cause any embarrassment to the people concerned when this has happened recently, but it is clearly undesirable that anyone should be permitted to play without making proper applications. The orchestra is always anxious to encourage promising young players, and there may be no objection to them playing as student members at early rehearsals in the string section, provided they make proper application to do so.

"In the wind section, however, balance – which has been the subject of some public criticism – is upset by the doubling of odd parts, and in future Mr Iliffe will have to insist that no wind parts shall be "doubled" even at rehearsal, without his specific instructions."

The news of the death of Sir Malcolm Sargent in October 1967 caused great sadness in the

Sir Malcolm Sargent - one of the last photos taken before his death in 1967. Sir Malcolm was knighted in 1947.

LSO as there were still many players in the orchestra who had performed under his baton. Although Sargent hadn't conducted the orchestra for more than twenty years, he was its president and always remained interested in its activities. In fact he wrote to the orchestra in 1963 to express his delight that, after forty years, Leicester Corporation had, at long last, recognised its value as a cultural asset by awarding it an annual grant.

A Sargent Memorial Concert was arranged for December 5, 1967 with Cyril Smith and Phyllis Sellick as the piano soloists. As close personal friends of Sargent, the choice of this popular husband and wife team was particularly apt. They played Mozart's Concerto in E flat for two pianos, K.365. Nimrod from Elgar's Enigma Variations opened the concert, which

LSO at the De Montfort Hall in April 1968 with Simeon Iliffe on the rostrum.

featured other Sargent favourites: Mendelssohn's Ruy Blas Overture, his own arrangement of Borodin's Nocturne from the String Quartet No.2, Sullivan's Overture to the Yeomen of the Guard and Schubert's Unfinished Symphony. There was a full house and according to RAP, orchestra and conductor "were at their best". It was a moving occasion and a heartfelt farewell to the orchestra's founding father and one of the country's most popular conductors.

Another great British conductor, Sir John Barbirolli, agreed to succeed Sargent as the president of the LSO. He was the renowned head of the Halle Orchestra who loved the De Montfort Hall and appeared there with the Halle several times each season. His popularity in Leicester knew no bounds and his appearances almost always meant a capacity audience. Sadly, Barbirolli lived less than three years longer than Sargent and in August 1970, the LSO was in search of yet another president. This time, it was decided to opt for a well-known local personality rather than a famous musician and there was one very obvious contender, the local industrialist and benefactor of the city's music library, Dr Mac Goldsmith. Over recent seasons, Dr Goldsmith had taken a great interest in the orchestra and had provided help both financially and in the form of advice. He became the orchestra's president in April 1971.

The choice of Mac Goldsmith was an inspired one. He was a man of ideas who got things done and was actively involved in many aspects of the running of the orchestra. He took genuine pride in the LSO's achievements and was a generous patron.

Another significant event of the late 1960s was the far-sighted appointment of Keith Smith

THE ORCHESTRA

President : SIR JOHN BARBIROLLI

First Violins
Mary Thornley *(leader)*
George Abrahams
Doreen Adnett
John Adnett
Maud Bown
Eric Cusworth
Celia Davies
Maurice Dilley
Christine Greer
Gilbert Holmes
Cicely Kibart
Donald Macdonald
Jessica McEwen
Irene McMillan
Joyce Mountney
Lilian Pooley
Reginald Rudd

Second Violins
Stella Shield *(leader)*
Gertrude Cooper
Mary Gaffney
Dianne Garner
Shirley Gladstone
Arthur Hames
Sarah Leese
George Middleton
Robert Pepperday
Janet Proctor
Aileen Shelton
Madge Stafford
Joseph Stackhouse
Irene Roberts
Elizabeth Smith
Sara Wyche

Violas
Cynthia Midgley *(leader)*
Nellie Bosisto
Yvonne Evans
Edward Freer
Thomas Freeston
John Fryer
Mollie Gooud
Irene Kemp
Julian Mustoe
Cyril Perfect

Cellos
Clifford Mansfield *(leader)*
Allen Bosworth
John Coney
Oliver Holmes

Cellos—continued
Haydn Hopkins
Tadeusz Kucharczyk
Judith Moon
Geoffrey Morton
Hilary Unna

Double Basses
Laurence Bradshaw *(leader)*
Gerald Bellamy
Alan Dunkley
Cecil Henson
Edna Lake
Lena Leighton
Lionel Madden
Graham Tomkinson

Flutes
Charles Quarmby
Ernest Smith

Oboes
Thelma Marion
David Angrave

Clarinets
Arthur Field
Ralph Whiteman

Bassoons
Donald Gimson
Jeremy Heal

Horns
Leonard Hartopp
Martin Gilding
David Foulds
Peter Bateman

Trumpets
Alan Whitehead
John Baugh
Malcolm Thompson
Roland Johnson

Trombones
Clifford Hutt
Barrie Lee
Nicholas Cooper

Tuba
Terence Weston

Timpani
Phyllis de Mond

Percussion
Michael Moore

Chairman : Arthur Thornley
Hon. Secretary : E. D. Smith
Assistant Hon. Secretary : Mrs. Irene McMillan
Hon. Treasurer : Mrs. Stella Shield
Orchestral Steward : Michael Moore.

LSO player list from April 1968.

as the orchestra's deputy conductor. He was to play an important role in the LSO's life for more than a quarter of a century.

By the early 1970s, some of those who had been eager to see Simeon Iliffe appointed were beginning to call for a younger man on the rostrum. They cited a limited repertoire, dwindling audiences and an ageing orchestra. Iliffe himself was now in his eighties and many of the older orchestral players were his personal friends. There was a joke amongst local musicians to the effect that the main qualification needed to play in the Leicester Symphony Orchestra was to be over fifty years old. Amongst the younger music lovers, the LSO was seen as stuffy and old fashioned.

Arthur Thornley, Dr Mac Goldsmith (LSO president), Mrs Ruth Goldsmith and Simeon Iliffe at an LSO function in November 1971.

It was unfair to blame Iliffe for all the orchestra's troubles however. The style of the advertising was contributing to the overall impression. The design of posters and handbills hadn't changed for years and the printed programmes also had a dated air about them. By this time the Leicester Philharmonic Choir, for example, was producing attractive, colourful programmes and advertising material that made the LSO's efforts appear very dowdy.

Things took a turn for the better in the orchestra's Golden Jubilee season of 1972-1973. The jubilee concert itself, held on November 28, 1972, had an impressive gold covered programme with numerous photographs and a short history of the orchestra written by Arthur Thornley. The event was a great success. Iliffe and the

Cover of concert programme November 1972

orchestra were on splendid form and there was a large and enthusiastic audience. The soloist was the great Russian pianist, Shura Cherkassky and the programme consisted of Wagner's Overture to Die Meistersinger, Tchaikovsky's Piano Concerto No. 1 in B flat minor and Dvorak's

Symphony No. 7 in D minor.

Critical opinion was encouraging. Cherkassky was "magnificent" and Iliffe's account of the Dvorak was considered robust and powerful. The orchestral playing was confident and accurate despite the occasional "coarse" moment in the brass. Generally, the jubilee celebrations were a happy time for the orchestra and its management.

The season continued on February 13, 1973 with an ambitious programme that concluded with another performance of Mahler's First Symphony, which was described as "a brave effort which gave much pleasure despite anxious moments". For the final concert on April 5, Cyril Smith and Phyllis Sellick were the guest artists in a very well received programme consisting of Walton's Crown Imperial, Saint-Saens' Carnival of the Animals, Malcolm Arnold's Concerto for Phyllis and Cyril, and Mendelssohn's Italian Symphony. The Arnold concerto was a real showstopper and the jazz inspired final movement had to be repeated before the audience would allow the concert to continue. The Golden Jubilee season was also a welcome financial success, and for the first time for many years the orchestra was in the fortunate position of having an excess of income over expenditure.

Eighty-five-year-old Mr. Simeon Iliffe, who has retired as conductor of the Leicester Symphony Orchestra, is seen (right) during the rehearsal for tonight's concert at the De Montfort Hall, being presented with an inscribed silver tray by Mr. E. D. Smith, secretary of the Orchestra in appreciation of his long services.

Ernest Smith (left) LSO secretary, presents Simeon Iliffe with an inscribed silver tray in appreciaion of his long and dedicated service to the orcehstra in May 1972.

Simeon Iliffe continued as conductor for another season, directing amongst other things Tchaikovsky's Romeo and Juliet Overture, Don Gillis's Symphony for Fun, Dvorak's New World Symphony and the Symphony in D minor by Cesar Franck. However by the summer of 1974 the eighty-five year old, who fifteen years earlier was persuaded to "fill in for a season until someone younger can be found", decided to retire. He had served the orchestra well and could look back on his fifteen years as its conductor with pride. It was a period of progress and solid achievement. He had been an important figure in the LSO for more than half a century.

His successor was waiting in the wings.

11. Keith Smith Takes Over

The Leicester Symphony Orchestra had appointed Keith Smith as deputy conductor in 1968 and six years on he had made quite a name for himself on the local musical scene.

Already established as the inspiring chorus master of the Leicester Philharmonic Choir and founder conductor of the Wigston Civic Orchestra, Keith Smith was in many ways an obvious choice as Iliffe's successor. He had been a violinist in the LSO since 1964 and his musical credentials were impressive. Like his predecessor he was a local man having been born in Wigston and educated at Kibworth Beauchamp Grammar School. His musical career began at the age of six when he took private piano and singing lessons. As a boy treble he won many prizes and awards for singing and was a regular competitor at music festivals. In later years he played in both the Leicestershire Schools Symphony Orchestra and the National Youth Orchestra.

The Leicestershire Schools Symphony Orchestra had been founded in 1948 by Eric Pinkett, the youthful and charismatic county schools Director of Music. With the enthusiastic backing of Stewart Mason, the Director of Education for Leicestershire, Pinkett quickly turned his orchestra into a nationally acclaimed ensemble that attracted musicians of the calibre of Sir Michael Tippett, Norman del Mar and Sir Arthur Bliss. Recordings by the LSSO as it was known, made in the 1960s and 70s, illustrate the quality of the orchestra. Many players on those recordings went on to join leading British orchestras and some, including its future conductor, joined the Leicester Symphony Orchestra, which, as a consequence, also became a beneficiary of Pinkett's thorough training.

After leaving school, Keith Smith took a degree in music at Leeds University and followed this with a course in choral and orchestral conducting at the Royal College of Music where he conducted the Royal College Polyphonic Choir. Later he became a music teacher at Guthlaxton School in Wigston. At this time he founded the Wigston Civic Orchestra and became the deputy Conductor of the LSO where he took rehearsals for the string section. In later years, Smith became Director of Music at Banbury School and conductor of the Southampton Youth Orchestra which he led with considerable success for a quarter of a century.

The first concert under the new permanent conductor was on November 6, 1974 and the programme consisted of the Prelude and Liebstod from Wagner's Tristan and Isolde, Lalo's Symphony Espagnole with Alfredo Campoli, Symphony No. 5 in D major by Vaughan Williams and to finish, the Festival Overture by Shostakovich.

Already, there is a difference in programme planning. Until Smith's arrival the Vaughan

The LSO with new conductor Keith Smith, taken in 1975.

Williams and Shostakovich would have been considered too risky, but these were works with which the new conductor had a strong affinity. The standard classics continued to appear but these were interspersed with more twentieth century items and there was less emphasis on popular crowd pullers.

The concert was well received and the orchestra coped ably with the unfamiliar works. The headline in the Leicester Mercury was Leicester Symphony's New Conductor in Auspicious Debut. Ralph Pugsley stated that Smith "displayed an authoritative style, a clear and flexible stick technique and, most important of all, an excellent sense of performance". In view of a misunderstanding, Campoli played only three of the five movements of Lalo's Symphony Espagnole, which was a pity as the standard of his playing was "marvellous". The Vaughan Williams was given a "very acceptable" performance with Pugsley remarking, even at this early stage, on the fact that Keith Smith had a natural affinity with English music, as he displayed "evident sympathy for the work and a close understanding of its reassuring philosophy". The opening Wagner item was well sustained despite "one or two moments of doubt" and the closing Shostakovich overture was "full of the thrill of excitement". There was indeed a sense of excitement about the whole evening that promised great things for the future, as was the case in earlier years with the arrival of both Harry Shaw and Simeon Iliffe.

At the final rehearsal for Keith Smith's first concert, Simeon Iliffe was presented with an inscribed silver salver by another long serving stalwart of the orchestra, Ernest Smith. As the LSO's secretary, Smith worked alongside Arthur Thornley for many years. He had made it a

The Orchestra

First Violins
Mary Thornley (*leader*)
Doreen Adnett
John Adnett
Maud Bown
Jennifer Boston
Bryan Brown
Eric Cusworth
Christine Greer
Cicely Kibart
Irene McMillan
Joyce Mountney
Lilian Pooley
Robert Pepperday
Reginald Rudd
Joseph Stackhouse
Madge Stafford

Second Violins
Stella Shield (*leader*)
Kathryn Aiers
Josephine Bedford
Arthur Hames
Leslie Howe
Christine Jarman
George Middleton
Rodney Newman
Antony Poll
Irene Roberts
Aileen Shelton
Helen Smith
Geoffrey Tomlinson
Margaret West
Linda Whitehead
Robin Whittle
Jerzy Wieczorek
Anne Wright

Violas
Sandy Hunt (*leader*)
Desirée Cunningham
Edward Freer
Thomas Freestone
Robert Gallacher
Helen Leech
Judith Newell
Stephanie Russell
Caroline Smith
Janet West

Cellos
Haydn Hopkins (*leader*)
Ian Harkis
Allen Bosworth
Roger Clarke
Jack Coney
Andrew Fuller
Roger Hides
Clifford Mansfield
Patrick Micel
Julia Mobbs
Geoffrey Morton
Malcolm Roe

Double Basses
Gerald Bellamy (*leader*)
Cecil Henson
Arthur Sharp
Christine Smith
Susan Stops
Graham Tomkinson

Flutes
Jennifer Brooks
Ernest Smith
Katharine White

Oboes
David Angrave
Kathryn Byrne
Kathleen Newman

Cor Anglais
Kathryn Byrne

Clarinets
Ralph Whiteman
Robert Greenlees

Bassoons
Donald Gimson
Christine Medlock

Contra Bassoon
Christopher Wykes

Horns
Leonard Hartopp
Martin Gilding
Charles Smith
David Wilde

Trumpets
John Baugh
Malcolm Thompson

Trombones
Clifford Hutt
Barrie Lee
Jack Wright

Tuba
Terence Weston

Timpani
Phyllis de Mond

Percussion
Angela Boot
Colin Goldsmith
Robert Nutt
Helen Wood

Harps
Olga Weston
Kathryn Nightingale

LSO player list February 1975.

priority to increase the number of patrons and involve local businesses in sponsorship. He was successful in both aims and helped to put the orchestra on a much more secure financial footing. However, his talents were not just confined to administration, as he was one of the orchestra's most versatile musicians. An accomplished player of both the double bass and the flute, Smith was a visible presence at all LSO concerts for more than three decades, and after Thornley's

Cover of concert programme February 1976.

Keith Smith, baton raised, around 1978.

death, he ran the orchestra, with help, for many years. As Martin Gilding recalls, "The load shouldered by Ernest at that time was enormous and there was no one else with the urge or time to put in the necessary effort. Without him the orchestra could well have sunk when Arthur Thornley died." Ernest Smith worked tirelessly to promote the orchestra and was always concerned that it should be given the credit it deserved.

Keith Smith's early years with the LSO produced a welcome widening of the repertoire and a willingness to tackle unusual and sometimes difficult works. Understandably, the results were variable, but the policy gave the orchestra a strong sense of direction and happily, a number of younger players were seen in the ranks. As always, Smith was keen to give the young a chance, even if it meant taking a risk. There's no doubt that this was exactly the right policy as it was essential to attract young blood into the orchestra in order for it to survive into the twenty first century.

At this crucial time in the LSO's life, the critics were usually supportive, but there were occasional complaints of "rough edges" and a "lack of expression and phrasing". Not all players found Smith an easy conductor to follow, citing his occasionally ambiguous beat and tendency to "flail" when things did not go quite as he wanted. This sometimes transmitted a sense of panic to the players, which did not help ensemble or expressive phrasing. However, when things went well, as they usually did, the orchestra played with real enthusiasm, commitment and new-found energy and excitement.

Not long into Keith Smith's reign the orchestra suffered a tragic loss in the death of Arthur Thornley, the man who had done more than anyone else to ensure the Leicester Symphony Orchestra survived into the twenty first century. Of all the musicians associated with the orchestra, none deserves more admiration. It would in fact be no exaggeration to say that without Thornley's outstanding diplomatic skills and absolute determination, the Leicester Symphony Orchestra would not have survived. He was at various times its honorary general secretary, chairman, conductor, oboist and percussion player.

THE LEICESTER SYMPHONY ORCHESTRA

President : Dr. M. Goldsmith
Vice-President : Dr. R. Meikle

A MEMORIAL CONCERT
TO THE LATE
ARTHUR THORNLEY

CONDUCTOR
KEITH SMITH

SOLOIST
JACK BRYMER
(CLARINET)

DE MONTFORT HALL   LEICESTER
Thursday, 2nd February, 1978

Cover of concert programme for the memorial concert to the late Arthur Thornley in 1978, autographed by Jack Brymer.

But his talent did not stop there. He was also the orchestra's chronicler and wrote numerous articles about its history and personalities. On top of this he was responsible for producing the programme and writing the programme notes.

Arthur Thornley was born in Leicester and educated at the Wyggeston Boys School where he showed both his musical prowess and his organisational skills by founding the first school orchestra. He was a printer by profession, but his heart was in music. He joined the LSO in its very early days. Initially he was an oboist, but it was not long before he was appointed the orchestra's honorary secretary. Sargent had the highest regard for him both as musician and administrator. As we have seen, during the crucial period of Sargent's long and serious illness, he was the vital and trusted link between conductor and orchestra.

During the difficult days of the Second World War, he kept the orchestra going almost single-handedly by acting as conductor, administrator and impresario. At this time he was described by Ernest Gorham Gee as "the finest amateur musician in Leicester". Later he became the LSO's chairman and was successful in obtaining civic funding as well as private support. Even in the season before his death he was active in trying to raise more funds for his beloved LSO and on the day he died he was involved in scoring a work for the orchestra's next concert, as well as making plans for its future.

Although primarily associated with the Leicester Symphony Orchestra, Arthur Thornley was also involved in the wider musical life of the city. He had a great love of opera and was instrumental in setting up the Leicester Opera Club. He was their conductor and musical arranger. This latter activity required hours of painstaking work in adapting large scores for small orchestra. His thorough knowledge of instrumentation and orchestral balance were invaluable in this sphere and his arrangements were so practical that they are used to this day.

Another of Thornley's valuable contributions to the city's cultural life was his Leicester Winter Diary in which every event of importance in musical, literary and artistic life of the city were recorded. Each society had its programme listed and there was a day by day chronological reminder of what the season held. It was published by Thornley's own company in Bowling Green Street, Leicester.

A memorial concert to Arthur Thornley took place in the De Montfort Hall on Thursday 2 February 1978. The guest artist was the great clarinettist, Jack Brymer and the programme included Thornley's own arrangement of Bach's Toccata and Fugue in D minor, Bizet's Carmen Suite, Mozart's Clarinet Concerto and Schubert's Unfinished Symphony. A spoken appreciation was given by his old friend, Archie Orton.

Over the middle years of the last century, there were times when, were it not for Arthur Thornley's boundless energy, enthusiasm and conviction, Leicester's strong and distinguished tradition of amateur orchestral playing and operatic performance could all too easily have disappeared.

12. *Progress and Competition*

As the seventies drew on, the orchestra made steady progress and maintained its relatively small but loyal audience. There was, as always, a determination to stick to the huge De Montfort Hall which, in the days before raked seating reduced the capacity, made an audience of two to five hundred people look tiny. This did not help morale and meant that some concerts had very little atmosphere, but in reality, there was no other hall in the city that was suitable for full-scale symphony concerts. However, despite these problems, programmes under Keith Smith had an adventurous quality that was very refreshing. Milhaud, Butterworth, Chaminade, Malcolm Williamson, Delius and Mahler appeared alongside the more familiar Beethoven, Brahms, Dvorak and Tchaikovsky.

Reports on the concerts from the Leicester Mercury's team of critics remained largely encouraging. In November 1976, Peter Crump was full of praise for a performance of Tchaikovsky's Fifth Symphony that had "passion in every climax and tenderness in every caressing phrase". The following year, Ralph Pugsley found Smith's account of Dvorak's Eighth Symphony "very enjoyable". At two concerts within a year of each other at the end of the 1970s, the orchestra is praised for its "accurate ensemble" and "electric performance" in The Roman Carnival Overture and "driving force" in Saint Saens' Third Symphony. Five months later, Wagner's Meistersinger Overture and Delibes' Sylvia ballet music "were played with style and careful detail". In a much appreciated performance of Milhaud's Concerto for Marimba and Vibraphone, ensemble between soloist, Heather Corbett, and orchestra "could not be faulted" and great praise was given to the orchestra for being "bold and different" in programming such an unusual work.

Keith Smith's professional background as a teacher and his desire to encourage the young, both as players and listeners, led to the staging of a Saturday morning family concert with the title: A Musical Guide to the Orchestra. This took place on April 29, 1978, and was the first specially devised children's concert the LSO had given since the days of Malcolm Sargent. The programme included works by Strauss, Mozart, Suppe, Vaughan Williams, Verdi, Haydn and Arnold and there were four soloists – all brass players: Martin Kelly (trombone), Paul Marsden (trumpet), Dave Powell (tuba) and Phil Walker (horn). The concert was billed as an event "for Children and Parents" and in order to have the widest possible appeal, all the seats were priced at 75p.

This extra concert can now be see as one of the first attempts for some years to widen the orchestra's horizons and to reach out to a different audience. The staging of special events is not always easy for amateur orchestras as players' time is limited. Time for practice has to be found and concerts have to be rehearsed but since the late 1970s the LSO has managed many successful extra events.

In the last year of the decade, the orchestra was joined by the Leicester Philharmonic Choir for a performance of Beethoven's Ninth Symphony. It was described by Peter Crump in the Leicester Mercury as "an historic occasion" and he found the choir "did better than the orchestra, managing Beethoven's great demands with aplomb". He felt the orchestra was better in Mendelsshohn's Ruy Blas Overture and Mozart's Oboe Concerto.

A year or so later on January 31, 1980 the Master of the Queen's Music, Malcolm Williamson, appeared as soloist in his own piano concerto. Williamson was a friend of Keith Smith and it was quite an event to get so distinguished a musician to perform one of his own works with the orchestra. The concert was well received. Critic Peter Crump, himself an accomplished pianist and composer, considered it "an event of great importance". He described Williamson's concerto as "busy, bustling and extrovert" and its construction as "occasionally clumsy", but said that it was played with panache and accompanied with remarkable skill: "Top marks to Keith Smith and the orchestra for being equal to the occasion and providing just the right kind of aplomb."

The other items in this significant concert drew praise from Crump: "Weber's Oberon Overture and the utterly charming The Banks of Green Willow by George Butterworth showed exactly what the orchestra, particularly the strings, can do." He concludes by saying: "There seems to be emerging a particular Leicester Symphony Orchestra sound, as unmistakable as a fingerprint."

There were occasional comments of Smith's inconsistent style of interpretation. When inspired, he could produce very impressive performances, but sometimes both orchestra and conductor seemed lacklustre, as in Beethoven's Egmont Overture which was described as "tentative and lacking in steam". A performance of the same composer's Fidelio overture in the following season was described by another critic as "pedestrian". However at this same concert, the following piece, Butterworth's rhapsody A Shropshire Lad, was "played with real sensitivity". A performance of Beethoven's Pastoral Symphony in 1980, "suffered from Keith Smith's wayward tempi" and Wagner's Lohengrin Act 3 Prelude was pushed so hard that "rhythmic precision was sacrificed". Again, still in the same concert, Elgar's Pomp and Circumstance March No. 4 "was undermined by the hesitancy of the big tune". In a 1981 summer concert held in Holy Cross Priory, the programme included Roussel's Le Festin D'Araignee (The Spider's Banquet) which was less than perfect as the Mercury made clear with a headline that stated, "Roussel was Dubious Choice for Concert", Peter Crump described the whole evening as "one of liveliness but also of unevenness of quality".

These observations are, on the whole, constructive and a sign that the orchestra was being stretched and challenged. And Peter Crump could be very generous in his praise, as he was after the Members' Summer Concert of June 14, 1980 when he wrote, "It was a new departure for the Leicester Symphony Orchestra conducted by Keith Smith to perform with reduced numbers at their concert at Holy Cross Priory on Saturday night. But it was crowned with success in more than one way.

"In the first place their high standard was amply maintained. Knowing Mr Smith's liking for fast tempos I was agog to know what would happen with Mozart's Magic Flute Overture and Beethoven's Fourth Symphony, both bristling with fast notes.

"What did happen was a performance both exciting and well controlled. As for Mozart's Horn Concerto K447, Martin Gilding, who is already deservedly known as a soloist, was well on top of the solo part with highly attractive tone.

"The interesting choice of Sibelius's Pelleas and Melisande Suite was well suited to the church's acoustics which are particularly kind to sustained tone and which brought out the best in the orchestra, particularly in the strings."

Peter Crump's final paragraph was reserved for the Priory itself: "This brings me to the second highly successful feature of this concert. That was the venue. Not only is this a church with excellent acoustics, but one which is welcoming to concert audiences without loss of reverence. I hope it will be a setting for more concerts like this."

The LSO invariably performed well when away from the vast space of the De Monfort Hall. Smaller venues bring the players closer to the audience and a more intimate atmosphere is created. Invariably "playing away" brought its own rewards – although it has to be said that in those days, it was a relatively rare occurrence.

On September 10, 1980, the Post Office issued a set of commemorative postage stamps depicting four famous British conductors; Sir Henry Wood, Sir Thomas Beecham, Sir Malcolm

First day cover 'Sir Malcolm Sargent - Leicester Symphony Orchestra' stamp issue, 10 September 1980. The sharp eyed will notice that the Sargent image on the franking is in fact laterally inverted. We are informed that this does not increase the value.

Sargent and Sir John Barbirolli. To coincide with this, Mr A G Bradbury, a local first day cover specialist arranged for a special Leicester Symphony Orchestra edition of 5,000 (in fact only 1,000 were produced) individually numbered covers to be issued. These displayed the full set of stamps which were franked with a pictorial handstamped postmark produced by the Post Office featuring a depiction of Sargent, in a classic pose, on a rostrum and reads, "The Leicester Symphony Orchestra celebrate their 57th year and honour their former conductor Sir Malcolm Sargent." The covers were posted in a special box in the De Montfort Hall and bore a distinctive cachet to that effect. The covers, which were advertised in the Leicester Mercury, cost £2.50 and came with their own protective envelope. These have now become collector's items and are seldom seen on the open market.

A highlight of the following season was the January 1981 concert which featured the Leicester Philharmonic Choir and the well-known local concert pianist and teacher, Marlene Fleet, who played Liszt's Piano Concerto No.1. The symphony was Schumann's 3rd (Rhenish) and the concert opened with Nicolai's overture to the Merry Wives of Windsor. The choir sang Parry's Blest Pair of Sirens and Elgar's From the Bavarian Highlands.

David Johnson, writing in the Leicester Mercury, gave the concert an enthusiastic review with the heading, "Romantic style suits City's Top Orchestra". He began, "On paper Saturday Night's Leicester Symphony Orchestra programme looked diverse and indigestible, but it turned out to be an enjoying and uplifting concert. Two features gave it a satisfying unity, the local background of all the participants and the grand romantic style of most of the music, culminating in a swaggering Elgar finale."

Johnson goes on to say the style of the music "suited the orchestra, who captured the broad comedy of Nicolai's overture... and the high spirits of Schumann's Rhenish Symphony." He thought Marlene Fleet offered a "restrained" account of the concerto that was impressive nonetheless and was pleased to see Smith in charge of both his orchestra and choir, although he thought the choir was "strangely underemployed". He liked what they did perform and concluded by saying: "There is scope here for greater co-operation between Leicester's chief orchestra and choir, in the large-scale but lesser-known works of the repertoire – some Vaughan Williams perhaps?"

At this time, Leicester Opera (formerly the Consort Musicale) was giving annual summer performances of light opera at the Haymarket Theatre in Leicester's city centre. The LSO was invariably asked to accompany these productions and although some members may have found summer rehearsals difficult to fit into holiday schedules, these events, usually spanning a week-end in June, proved a useful source of extra income for the orchestra. A much reduced LSO continued to play for Leicester Opera's annual winter productions which ran for a week in October at the Little Theatre.

The major event of the early eighties was the orchestra's Diamond Jubilee. The celebration concert took place on Thursday November 4, 1982 and the programme consisted of Walton's

Orchestra celebrate jubilee

60 years old, and still going strong

One of Leicester's most famous institutions, the Leicester Symphony Orchestra, celebrate their Diamond Jubilee this year — and in a style which one of its founders and conductors, the late Sir Malcolm Sargent, would have been proud.

World-famous cellist Julian Lloyd-Webber will be the star of a concert to be staged on November 4 at the venue which has been the orchestra's home for the past 60 years — the De Montfort Hall.

It was there, on October 24, 1922, after lengthy auditioning, that the Leicester Symphony Orchestra was born.

Malcolm Sargent, then organist at Melton Parish Church, conducted the 80-piece orchestra in front of a large audience.

The orchestra were formed with money provided by William "Billy" Russell and his son Karl, who ran a music shop on London Road, as a promotional exercise over their

main rivals, Herbert Marshall's, of Belvoir Street.

It worked extremely well. People flocked from miles around to hear the semi-professional outfit, one of few operating in the provinces.

Playing four or five concerts a season, Sargent occasionally took the role of solo pianist and organist for many of the works they played.

The benefit to Sargent and the orchestra was mutual, according to Mr. Robert Shaw, assistant secretary, responsible for organisation and administration.

His years with the orchestra acted as a springboard for the young Sargent's career.

In 1931 the orchestra hit a crisis. The Russells withdrew much of their financial interest and Sargent became ill.

But, said Mr. Shaw, mainly through the efforts of the late Arthur Thornley, husband of the leader Mrs. Mary Thornley, the orchestra remained in existence.

A London concert promoter helped to get them back on their feet and they merged with the Leicester Philharmonic Choir, a partnership which lasted until 1937.

Mrs. Thornley recalled that Sargent was a poor correspondent which made it difficult for her

by Alan Thompson

husband to get programme details settled.

Her husband appealed to Sargent who said: "Thornley, get on the train with me tomorrow morning, as far as Kettering, and we will get the four concerts arranged for next season."

"This happened on several occasions and it worked very well. Malcolm Sargent had an amazingly quick brain and 'a very pretty wit' to quote Gilbert and Sullivan," she said.

During the war years, although numbers dwindled, the orchestra continued and toured several military establishments. They were still attracting celebrated artists like Eva Turner.

By 1942, however, they were plunged back into crisis with the revival of another local orchestra and visits to the provinces by professional orchestras.

The orchestra could not continue to compete and went into mothballs for a year.

Once more, the orchestra hauled themselves back on to their feet and

KEITH SMITH

in later years, said Mr. Shaw, largely due to the help of benefactor Dr. Mac Goldsmith, after whom the Goldsmith Library in Belvoir Street is named, they remained in existence.

They were still attracting top names to concerts — and a string of top conductors.

At a cost of £2,000 to £3,000 to stage each concert, finance is still a problem.

But through local authority grants, benefactors and a growing number of patrons the orchestra are maintaining their position.

Mr. Shaw said: "The vast majority of members are dedicated amateurs, a lot of music teachers.

"Hopefully, the day will come when the LSO will be able to expand the number of concerts, possibly even out into the county and the range and scope of programmes."

The orchestra's conductor is Mr. Keith Smith, who joined them in 1973.

Sir Malcolm Sargent, six months before his death in 1967.

Leicester Mercury article to coincide with Diamond Jubilee (60 years) of LSO, in November 1982. Note how, on several occasions in Sargent's time, concerts were planned on the train between Leicester and Kettering.

Coronation March and Crown Imperial, Sargent's An Impression on a Windy Day, Elgar's Cello Concerto and Sibelius's Symphony No. 5. It was an ambitious programme especially as there would almost certainly be a full house and the concert was to be broadcast on local radio.

The choice of the Sibelius produced a few raised eyebrows among players and commentators. The reason for questioning its inclusion was a sound one: Why, when the orchestra is likely to have its largest audience for a decade, risk a difficult and to some players unfamiliar work, when the safer thing would have been to opt for a universally popular work, say Tchaikovsky's Fifth or Dvorak's New World Symphony? The concert was sure to be a showcase for the orchestra and to have it playing below its best would be unfortunate and possibly counter productive. However, objections were overridden and Sibelius's 5th duly appeared on the programme.

Predictions turned out to be true. The concert attracted a capacity audience and the Mercury's critic began his review by stating that he had rarely seen the De Montfort Hall so full. This, he thought, was a tribute to the orchestra's founder. Also, not surprisingly, the Sibelius proved to be less than an ideal work for such a conspicuous occasion. It was a rather tentative and underpowered account of a work that needs absolute confidence and accuracy. All the Leicester Mercury critic, Christopher Wood, said was that "it made tremendous demands on the orchestra". Some of those present felt it was a lost opportunity, as despite the full house, audience numbers at subsequent concerts did not improve, as they may have done had the orchestra turned in a more impressive performance of a work in which they felt more at ease.

The other works in the programme enjoyed greater success. Sargent's piece was performed with "pleasing tonal variety" and the Elgar Cello Concerto – described as "the great work of the evening" was played with "tremendous tone and technical mastery" by soloist Julian Lloyd Webber. A final paragraph in the review drew readers' attention to the fact that Mary Thornley had by this time, been playing in the orchestra for the whole of its sixty year existence and that for the last thirty-two of those years, she had been its leader.

The next concert in the Diamond Jubilee season featured the winner of the 1982 BBC Young Musician of the Year Competition, Anna Markland. She played the Grieg Piano Concerto and critical comment was favourable. "Well done Anna" was the opening sentence of Peter Crump's review in the Leicester Mercury. There was "classical attention to detail" in her reading and she was not put off by the orchestra's "inflexible, not to say relentless accompaniment". The concert opened with a "lively" account of the Benvenuto Cellini overture by Berlioz and closed with an "ambitious" performance of Pictures from an Exhibition.

Keith Smith and LSO in November 1982 during it's 60 year anniversary. Keith Smith joined the LSO as a violinist in April 1967. His first concert as conductor was November 1974 and his last, May 1995.

The March concert took the form of a memorial to Simeon Iliffe, the orchestra's former conductor, who had died the previous year at the age of ninety three. He had been described in his obituary in the Mercury as "Leicester's grand Old Man of Music". The programme consisted of Rossini's William Tell overture, The Perfect Fool ballet music by Holst, Glazounov's Violin Concerto

LEICESTER SYMPHONY ORCHESTRA
Permanent Conductor : Keith Smith

FIRST VIOLINS
Mary Thornley (Leader)
Doreen Adnett
John Adnett
John Aspinall
Alan Bett
Bryan Evans
Veronica Fletcher
Janet Gallacher
Anne Gosling
George Grand
Marie Hewes
Cicely Kibart
Suzanne Kilby
Robert Pepperday
Gillian Print
Michael Redman
Helen Smith
Morag Thomson
Geoffrey Tomlinson
John Wakefield
Robin Whittle

SECOND VIOLINS
Jill Bentley
Angela Bristow
Andrea Broughton
*Judith Busby
Helen Butler
Kim Butler
Lesley Calton
James Gibbons
Arthur Hames
Helen Johnson
Tracy Madelin
George Middleton
Jean Page
Roy E. Print
Karen Rouse
Sally Slater
Caroline Taylor
Shelagh Thomson
Linda Whitebread

VIOLAS
Thelma Bull
Frances Binding
Thomas Freestone
Robert Gallacher
Beryl Ginz
Oliver Hurst
Helen Leach
*Stephanie Mawby
Alwyn Pollard
Caroline Roberts
Michael Sackin

'CELLOS
Jack Coney
*.Haydn Hopkins
Susan Hinckley
Geoffrey Morton
William Preddy
Frances Prockter
Malcolm Roe
Richard Stephen
Megan Timpson
Nigel Willey
+ Pat Dobson

DOUBLE BASSES
*Gerald Bellamy
Arthur Sharp
Ernest Smith
Graham Tomkinson

FLUTES
*Jenny Brooks
Karen Hardy

OBOES
*Rosemary Greenless
Mandy Woolman

CLARINETS
*Paul Gray
Robert Greenless

BASSOONS
John Bagley
*Donald Gimson

HORNS
*Martin Gilding
Colin Harrison
Kay Johnson
Charles Smith

TRUMPETS
Richard Allen
* Alan Mawby

TROMBONES
David Cobble
Barrie Lee
*Michael Riley
John Scott

TUBA
Terence Weston

TIMPANI
Colin Goldsmith

PERCUSSION
Maurice Vann

HARP
Olga Briggs

* Indicates a Section Principal

Programme Notes compiled by Sheila James, John Hunt & R. J. Knight

DE MONTFORT HALL - LEICESTER
Forthcoming Events

Saturday, 13th November at 7.30 p.m.
Leicester City Council presents:
ROYAL DANISH ORCHESTRA
conductor: **Jerzy Semkow**

Nielsen : Helios Overture
Schumann : Piano Concerto
Tchaikovsky : Symphony No. 6
Soloist : **Stephen Bishop Kovacevich**
Tickets : £4; £3.75; £3.50; £3; £2.75; £2.50; £2; £1.75.

Saturday, 18th December at 7.30 p.m.
LEICESTER PHILHARMONIC SOCIETY
FESTIVAL OF CHRISTMAS MUSIC
In association with BBC Radio 2

BBC CONCERT ORCHESTRA
Conductor : **James Lockhart**
Soloists : **Valerie Masterson** (soprano)
John Treleaven (tenor)
Presenter : **John Craven**
Tickets : £3.90; £3.25; £2.75; £2.25; £2;
£1.75; £1.50.

On sale from Municipal Box Office, Town Hall Square, Leicester.

LSO player list November 1982.

Cover of concert programme from Diamond Jubilee season, March 30, 1983.

Leicester Mercury article from March 1983 - the memorial concert for Simeon Iliffe and Mary Thornley retiring as leader.

(with Phillipa Ibbotson), Bizet's Carmen Suite and Variations and Fugue on a Theme of Purcell (The Young Person's Guide to the Orchestra) by Benjamin Britten.

A warm tribute from Dr Robert Meikle, the orchestra's vice president, commented on Iliffe's versatility and all-round musicianship as well as his great personal qualities. The whole event was a worthy tribute to one of the orchestra's most significant figures. Surprisingly, this concert turned out to be the last with Mary Thornley as leader. She had held the post for thirty-three years and after an affectionate tribute by Keith Smith, the audience cheered. She intended to stay in the orchestra as a rank and file member. Her successor was Anne Gosling (later Hurst), a popular local player and teacher who in turn gave long and distinguished service to the LSO.

The most significant concert of the following season, and one which showed Smith and the orchestra at their best, was an all-English programme to mark the fiftieth anniversary of Elgar's death. Again, this was broadcast on local radio and consisted of two fanfares by Sir Arthur Bliss, the Fantasia on a Theme of Thomas Tallis by Vaughan Williams, Constant Lambert's Rio Grande and Elgar's First Symphony. In the performance of the Rio Grande, the orchestra was joined by the Leicester Philharmonic Choir.

The report was full of praise and described Smith's account of the Rio Grande as "spirited and precise" and the fine performance of Elgar's symphony was of a standard "to please Elgar himself". This concert and the many other performances of such works under Keith Smith's baton, showed the conductor to have a strong affinity and feeling for English music. Occasional inconsistencies there may have been in his performances of the mainstream Viennese classics, but as an interpreter of the English repertoire he produced fine, well considered readings that invariably pleased the critics.

LSO leader Anne Gosling (now Tupling), around 1983.

With an influx of new faces on the administrative side, a talented and lively young leader and the appointment of Robert Knight to the newly-created post of orchestra manager, the image of the LSO began to take on a more contemporary feel. Programmes were attractively designed and publicity became much more stylish. There was a big drive to find extra patrons and several new players were to be seen in the orchestra's ranks. Also it was around this time that the LSO became a limited company and a registered charity. Altogether, these changes gave the LSO a much higher profile in the musical life of the city.

Sadly, this did not translate into full houses, although there was a small improvement in attendance during the 1980s. However, in March 1985, the headline for Peter Crump's review read: "Poor Support For A Splendid Concert" and he began by saying: "A strong word of criticism is due to large numbers of potential audience members that stayed away from last night's concert." It could not have been due to the programme as it contained a popular assortment including Sibelius's Karelia Suite, Smetana's Vltava and Scheherazade by Rimsky-Korsakov. This curious phenomenon has been noticed throughout the orchestra's life. Even in the 1920s with Malcolm Sargent on the rostrum and a world famous soloist at his side, there could be rows of empty seats. On other occasions, and for no obvious reason, there was a full house.

One concert that did produce a large audience was given on November 8, 1984 in memory of the orchestra's recently deceased President, Dr Mac Goldsmith. A leading local industrialist, Goldsmith had fled to

Mary Thornley from the November 1982 programme.

England from Hitler's Germany in 1937. He arrived in Leicester soon after and became an important figure in the life of the city. His generosity helped music and many other causes such as healthcare, theatre, and education. He was made a Freeman of the City of Leicester and received an honorary doctorate from the university.

Undoubtedly the most active of figureheads, Mac Goldsmith had provided considerable financial help to the orchestra over a number of years and took a genuine interest in its affairs. He brought his considerable influence to bear on those he thought could be of help in any way. He and his wife Ruth could be seen at every LSO concert, quite often among a group of invited friends; brought along in the hope that they would be impressed enough to become patrons. His support, help and advice would be sorely missed.

Dr Goldsmith's Memorial Concert was an all Beethoven evening that began with the Ruins of Athens overture, then Peter Seivewright was the soloist in the Fourth Piano Concerto. Local concert pianist, Simon Lebens played the piano part in the Choral Fantasia with the university's Choral Society and the programme ended with the Fifth Symphony. Characteristically, the proceeds of the evening went to the Leicester Medical Research Foundation. Dr Goldsmith was succeeded as president by his wife who continued to support the orchestra in the same very practical and enthusiastic way. She attended almost every concert until her move to London in the spring of 2002 and continued to take a great interest in the orchestra's fortunes until her death in 2010 at the age of ninety four.

The LSO's programmes were showing remarkable imagination at this time. Robert Knight was not a professional musician but he had a vast knowledge of the repertoire and managed to persuade both conductor and other committee members to try a more adventurous programming policy. As a consequence, pieces performed in the mid to late eighties included Copland's Four Dance Episodes from Rodeo, Shostakovich's Second Piano Concerto, the first of De Falla's Three Cornered Hat suites, Poulenc's Organ Concerto, Respighi's Pines of Rome, Holst's Perfect Fool Ballet, Bernstein's Symphonic Dances from West Side Story, Milhaud's Le Boef sur le Toit and Stravinsky's Petrushka.

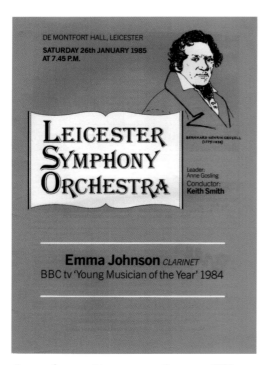

Cover of concert programme January 1985.

Popular favourites were not neglected and there were a number of "themed" evenings such as "A Night in Old Vienna", "A Gilbert and Sullivan Gala", "Family Fun and Favourites", "Brass meets Symphony" and "LSO Pops." There was a small but consistent increase in audience numbers which vindicated this more adventurous policy. However, with the resignation of Robert Knight from his post of Orchestral Manager and his departure from the Council of Management, there was a feeling that things could revert back to playing safe with unimaginative programmes and well-known soloists playing popular concertos.

Robert Knight had taken on an enormous task and carried it out with great enthusiasm and energy. However, there was a feeling that he had been overloaded with work and put under a lot of pressure, as most of the orchestra's administration along with front of house duties were part of his responsibility. These tasks were carried out in conjunction with his full-time job in the photographic industry. Consequently, it was decided to spread the workload between a number of volunteers rather than appoint another manager.

Fear of programmes losing their enterprising quality was unfounded and the orchestra continued to produce attractive and varied concerts. The Council of Management under the chairmanship of Dr Arthur Temple put a great deal of effort into promoting the orchestra while maintaining its more adventurous programme policy.

Publicity for LSO concert in May 1985.

Publicity for LSO concert February 1987.

Mercury review

Orchestra and audience in tune

IT is not often we get the opportunity to hear the Leicester Symphony Orchestra away from the De Montfort Hall but a gala concert was given in St. Paul's Parish Church in the West End of the City, and very interesting it proved to be.

Firstly, the orchestra seemed much less remote and a far better rapport between players and audience was established; consequently a good atmosphere prevailed throughout.

Also, despite some problems with seating, the orchestra sounded good and at close range we heard just how well it can play.

I hope this venture will be the first of many.

The programme opened with Schubert's Rosamunde overture and then four excellent horn soloists, Gary Koop, Martin Gilding, Roger Swann, and Julian Haslam, played Schumann's Konzertstuck for four horns and orchestra.

Exciting

It sounded confident and exciting particularly in the brilliant finale.

Keith Smith is a fine conductor of English music and Delius' Walk To the Paradise Garden had just the right yearning quality with some excellent woodwind playing.

In Mozart's Haffner Symphony, strings excelled with a clean and clear attack.

The performance was elegantly phrased and the conductor's hold on the impetuous finale was impressive.

A good standard of playing from all sections was heard in Brittens' colourful Soirees Musicales.

I am sure that this concert has won new and well-deserved support for the orchestra.

— Neil Crutchley

Leicester Mercury review of the LSO concert of June 24, 1988.

Some special events proved to be real crowd-pullers such as the Midsummer Concert given on 24 June 1988 in St. Paul's Church, Kirby Road in the west of the city. It was a beautiful summer evening and the orchestra was on good form. The varied programme: Schubert's Rosamunde Overture, Delius's The Walk to the Paradise Garden, Schumann's Concertstuck for Four Horns, Mozart's Haffner Symphony and Britten's Soirees Musicales, attracted a full house and the orchestra played well. The more intimate surroundings of St. Paul's drew conductor, players and audience closer together and there was an excellent atmosphere. It is a pity this event was not repeated as it was greatly enjoyed and met with strong critical approval.

Despite the very occasional sell-out, box office returns were a constant worry. As with many non-professional orchestras, the LSO was in a no-win situation. If it presented programmes that consisted entirely of popular items it would be accused of lack of enterprise and if it featured too many unusual or challenging works it would run the risk of box office disaster and the accusation of not catering for the ordinary music lover.

Another worrying factor at this time came in the form of competition. In 1986, a small orchestra was assembled by the local cellist, Andrew Constantine. Its first concert was a relatively low-key affair in a music room at Leicester University, but it soon became clear that Constantine and his Bardi Orchestra were not going to remain low-key for long.

Andrew Constantine had been the LSO's first-desk cellist for a short period, but he had wider ambitions. From his first concert, it was obvious that he was a gifted and technically competent conductor who very quickly attracted many of the city's best players and built up a large personal following. Before long the Bardi Orchestra was competing with the Leicester Symphony on its own ground, the De Montfort Hall.

There was no doubt that the Bardi with its polished presentation, high technical standards and strong sense of identity, made the LSO look rather dull and unexciting. On top of this, Constantine had become a nationally known figure as the winner of the first Donatella Flick conducting competition. The Bardi was performing on a regular basis in Birmingham's newly opened Symphony Hall as well as other venues around the country. Local audiences were significantly larger than those for the LSO. What was to be done? The Leicester Symphony was the city's own orchestra and it had a long and distinguished history. There was no question of disbanding, but how could it compete with its dynamic new rival? It was a difficult situation.

There was a fairly sizeable faction in the orchestra that felt it was time for a change of conductor. Keith Smith had been with the LSO for nearly twenty years and had served it well. But there were those amongst the orchestra's ranks who thought it was time for a change. They cited the fact that Smith did not seem popular with audiences and on many occasions barely managed two curtain calls. Furthermore, he no longer lived locally and was increasingly busy with commitments in the south of England where he enjoyed considerable success as the conductor of the City of Southampton Youth Orchestra. Standards in the LSO were not as high as they might have been and a number of players were beginning to find rehearsals less than enlightening.

Critics were also beginning to ask why the orchestra could not maintain its audience and occasionally made fairly outspoken remarks about the way things were going. For example, after a very poor house for a concert with a rag-bag of a programme that included Wagner's Good Friday Music from Parsifal, David Bedford's First Symphony and Schubert's Great C major Symphony, it was felt that the orchestra had let itself down by bad programme planning and lack of direction.

Bedford's symphony was described as "vibrant and colourful" and "notoriously difficult to play" but was "brought off with astonishing assurance". The Wagner was considered "hardly the most invigorating thing with which to start a concert" and although it was "well played" it was also "rather uncommitted". The Schubert symphony had a first movement that was "rushed and unidiomatic", a scherzo that "had little Viennese charm and was just too

Cover of concert programme April 1990.

A fine finale to concert season

THE Leicester Symphony Orchestra was on top form for its last De Montfort Hall concert of the season, which served to remind us that we should not take a local orchestra for granted, as it really can be a most impressive ensemble.

The high standard showed yet again what excellent local musicians we have in Leicester.

All sections played with distinction, both technically and in matters of expression.

Dvorak's 8th Symphony opened the concert, and after a rather cautious start, blossomed into a fine performance with plenty of dramatic contrast and lyrical charm.

The slow movement's delicate writing for strings and woodwind was perfectly realised with excellent balance and lightness of tone.

In the Finale, the variations were well contrasted, with lots of vigour.

Peter Cropper, the distinguished leader of the Lindsay Quartet, was the soloist in Elgar's Violin concerto, to which he brought passionate intensity and communication skills and, despite some tuning problems, gave a powerful performance.

– Neil Crutchley

Leicester Mercury review of concert, April 1990.

Cover of concert programme, September 1990.

hectic" and a finale in which "dynamic contrasts went for nothing - even the closing bars were bland". As if in justification for his remarks, the critic ended by saying: "The tepid applause was proof of this."

The early 1990s were in some ways a difficult time, but despite various worries, concerts still featured many interesting works. Bartok's Concerto for Orchestra appeared in the first programme of the decade and made great technical demands on the players. It was an enthusiastic, if rather rough-edged account of a twentieth century masterpiece. Peter Cropper, the renowned leader of the erstwhile Lindsay String Quartet was the soloist in April 1990. He played Elgar's Violin Concerto.

In June, a successful "Classical Pops" evening was given in Melton Mowbray. On September 15, a Battle of Britain memorial concert drew a large and appreciative audience to the De Montfort Hall. The programme was well suited to the occasion and included popular songs of the period alongside Walton's Spitfire Prelude and Fugue, the London Suite and the Dam Busters March, both by Eric Coates, Addinsell's Warsaw Concerto and the RAF March by Walford Davies.

A collaboration with the Leicester Philharmonic Choir in a concert featuring popular operatic, sacred and orchestral items was a highlight of 1991. Its mixture, including The Yeoman of the Guard Overture, the Anvil Chorus from Il Trovatore, the Chorus of the Hebrew Slaves from Nabucco, the Grand

March from Aida, Mozart's Oboe Concerto and Arnold's Scottish Dances, proved to be both an artistic and financial success.

An otherwise good performance of Elgar's Second Symphony in the same year was compromised by the omission of most of the percussion part. Instead of a timpanist and four other percussionists, the work was performed with a timpanist and one other, rather timid, player. As the critic of the time said in his review in the Leicester Mercury, "What a pity this potentially fine performance was, at the emotional high point of each movement (where Elgar underpins the orchestra with bass drum and cymbals) let down by a percussion section that was at best reticent and at worst, missing altogether". There were many who felt the orchestra had been shown to be unprofessional by playing the work without the correct complement of percussion players. Sadly, the reason for the problem was that an experienced percussion player pulled out at the last minute and the conductor had had no time to organise a substitute.

This perceived, but not always justified, cavalier attitude to the composer's wishes played into the hands of the orchestra's critics and gave ammunition to those who were calling for a change of conductor. However, with reference to the previous comments, it could be argued that Smith was the first conductor of the LSO since Sargent who was prepared to include the Elgar symphonies in his programmes and his enterprise was to be admired rather than criticised. Furthermore, missing percussion apart, Smith's Elgar interpretations were highly regarded by local critics who considered him to be a sensitive and enlightened interpreter of English music.

The next season saw a commercial success in April 1992, with "Springtime in Vienna"; a lightweight programme of Viennese delights spanning two centuries. These evenings based on a theme were proving to be a good way of ensuring a relatively large audience and good box office returns. More challenging musically, had been the February concert which included a performance of Dvorak's rarely heard Violin Concerto and Stravinsky's Firebird Suite.

Due to the refurbishment of the De Montfort Hall, the orchestra had to find alternative accommodation for the 1993-1994 season. After a long search, the 1,000 seat Evangelical Christian Centre, at Hesed House on Frog Island, was chosen and despite reservations it proved to be a good choice. An American Evening held there on February 19, 1994 attracted a capacity audience with a programme that included Copland's Clarinet Concerto and Menotti's prelude to Amelia Goes To The Ball, along with the ever popular American in Paris and dances from West Side Story. In April, the orchestra gave an all Russian evening at the same venue that included Shostakovich's Festive Overture and Glazounov's rarely heard Symphony No. 6. Both these concerts displayed imagination in programme planning. The American Evening was a good combination of the familiar and less well known and the Russian Evening gave a Leicester audience a very rare chance to hear a live performance of a symphony by Glazounov.

The November 1994 concert had to be cancelled due to a delay in the re-opening of the

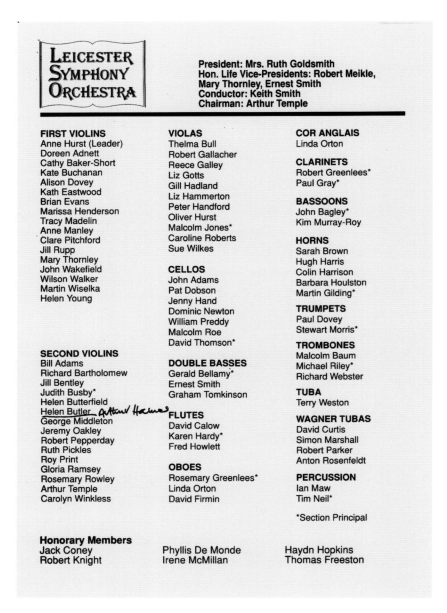

LEICESTER SYMPHONY ORCHESTRA

President: Mrs. Ruth Goldsmith
Hon. Life Vice-Presidents: Robert Meikle,
Mary Thornley, Ernest Smith
Conductor: Keith Smith
Chairman: Arthur Temple

FIRST VIOLINS
Anne Hurst (Leader)
Doreen Adnett
Cathy Baker-Short
Kate Buchanan
Alison Dovey
Kath Eastwood
Brian Evans
Marissa Henderson
Tracy Madelin
Anne Manley
Clare Pitchford
Jill Rupp
Mary Thornley
John Wakefield
Wilson Walker
Martin Wiselka
Helen Young

SECOND VIOLINS
Bill Adams
Richard Bartholomew
Jill Bentley
Judith Busby*
Helen Butterfield
Helen Butler_ Arthur Holmes
George Middleton
Jeremy Oakley
Robert Pepperday
Ruth Pickles
Roy Print
Gloria Ramsey
Rosemary Rowley
Arthur Temple
Carolyn Winkless

VIOLAS
Thelma Bull
Robert Gallacher
Reece Galley
Liz Gotts
Gill Hadland
Liz Hammerton
Peter Handford
Oliver Hurst
Malcolm Jones*
Caroline Roberts
Sue Wilkes

CELLOS
John Adams
Pat Dobson
Jenny Hand
Dominic Newton
William Preddy
Malcolm Roe
David Thomson*

DOUBLE BASSES
Gerald Bellamy*
Ernest Smith
Graham Tomkinson

FLUTES
David Calow
Karen Hardy*
Fred Howlett

OBOES
Rosemary Greenlees*
Linda Orton
David Firmin

COR ANGLAIS
Linda Orton

CLARINETS
Robert Greenlees*
Paul Gray*

BASSOONS
John Bagley*
Kim Murray-Roy

HORNS
Sarah Brown
Hugh Harris
Colin Harrison
Barbara Houlston
Martin Gilding*

TRUMPETS
Paul Dovey
Stewart Morris*

TROMBONES
Malcolm Baum
Michael Riley*
Richard Webster

TUBA
Terry Weston

WAGNER TUBAS
David Curtis
Simon Marshall
Robert Parker
Anton Rosenfeldt

PERCUSSION
Ian Maw
Tim Neil*

*Section Principal

Honorary Members
Jack Coney
Robert Knight

Phyllis De Monde
Irene McMillan

Haydn Hopkins
Thomas Freeston

LSO player list November 1992.

De Montfort Hall. It was to have consisted of Tchaikovsky's Romeo and Juliet Overture, Rodrigo's Concierto De Aranjuez and Elgar's Enigma Variations.

The 1994-1995 season turned out to be Keith Smith's last. He had been the orchestra's permanent conductor for twenty years, a record equalled only by Dr Malcolm Sargent. During his successful tenure he broadened the orchestra's outlook by introducing many new and attractive works and by encouraging younger players, soloists and administrators. The orchestra had improved its image and its business acumen. It also became a limited company.

The season's programmes had the characteristic Smith stamp and included some challenging and unusual works such as Ginastera's ballet suite Estancia, Wagner's Rienzi Overture and de Falla's Three Cornered Hat. There was another performance of Sibelius' Fifth Symphony and a well received account of Glazounov's Violin Concerto with Nicola Loud as soloist.

Not until the 1995-1996 season's programmes had been finalised and published did Smith indicate his wish to relinquish his position. Other conducting engagements made rehearsals for LSO concerts difficult to fit in and there was overseas work to consider. A meeting was held and an announcement was made and Smith, who had many close friends in the orchestra, accepted the honorary title of Conductor Emeritus in recognition of two decades of dedicated service that saw the LSO blossom into an orchestra ready to enter the new millennium.

Initially, Smith's departure caused a certain amount of worry, with the need to find three conductors for the rapidly approaching season. However, it did provide an opportunity to advertise the post and to find the right person for the 1996-1997 season. There was a huge response to the advertisement, which is a significant reminder of how times had changed since Simeon Iliffe had to be almost forced into the post in 1959.

Out of nearly forty candidates, six were chosen to attend auditions the following May. Meanwhile, conductors for the coming concerts needed to be found. Fortunately for the LSO, the Leicestershire County Symphony Orchestra had recently held auditions for a new conductor to replace the long-serving Clifford Hutt. There had been a good response and three of the candidates were offered concerts with the LSO. Those chosen were Roland Melia, Andrew Shulman and Ivor Setterfield. This sense of competition ensured that their concerts attracted significantly larger De Montfort Hall audiences than the LSO had known for some time.

Melia was first to appear on November 23, 1995 and his programme included Malcolm Sargent's own composition, An Impression on a Windy Day" performed to commemorate the former LSO conductor's centenary. Also in the programme were Elgar's Cello Concerto and Tchaikovsky's Fifth Symphony.

The concert was a great success. The orchestra played extremely well and the tone had a noticeable refinement. The players liked Melia and the review in the Leicester Mercury was full of praise for Melia's "clear beat and unruffled platform manner" as well as his ability to inspire the players. Only ten days prior to the LSO's account of the Tchaikovsky symphony, the Helsinki Philharmonic had performed the same work in the De Montfort Hall with "resounding success". However it was thought the LSO "acquitted themselves with distinction in a well projected, vigorous performance with sensible speeds and a refreshing lack of sentimentality".

Melia was followed on February 8, 1996, by Andrew Shulman, who was already well known

ESTER MERCURY, MONDAY, NOVEMBER 27, 1995 **19**

NG MUSICAL FARE

Tchaikovsky performed to perfection

Leicester Symphony Orchestra at De Montfort Hall.
Review: Neil Crutchley

AFTER the resounding success of the Helsinki Orchestra's performance of Tchaikovsky's Fifth Symphony in De Montfort Hall just 10 days ago, the Leicester Symphony Orchestra had a lot to live up to when they performed the same work in the same place on Thursday.

As it happened they acquitted themselves with distinction. Playing under an obviously well-liked guest conductor, the symphony was given a well projected vigorous performance with sensible speeds and a refreshing lack of sentimentality.

CLASSICAL

Roland Melia has a clear beat and an unruffled platform manner and the orchestra responded to him with real commitment. He had the score in his head rather than his head in the score and thus maintained eye contact with the players. Consequently there was a notable confidence in all departments.

There was a good sharp attack, well-built climaxes and a strong sense of line and phrase and, apart from a slight tendency to raucousness in the brass department, the overall sound was well integrated.

Robert Max was an exemplary soloist in Elgar's Cello Concerto, giving a seamless and lyrical reading of great technical assurance and, despite the odd moment of poor tuning, the accompaniment was well handled.

Malcolm Sargent's spritely Impression on a Windy Day opened the concert, which was given to mark his centenary and in aid of his cancer fund for children. It was a worthy tribute.

Leicester Mercury review of Roland Melia's first concert with LSO, November 1995.

as a professional cellist. His concert included two works that were on the cancelled November 1994 programme: Tchaikovsky's Romeo and Juliet Fantasy Overture and Elgar's Enigma Variations. It was a less distinguished evening than Melia's, with "moments of shaky ensemble and intonation" in the Tchaikovsky, which was described as "lacking dynamic contrast and drama". The Elgar fared better, but was also marred by "inaccuracies of ensemble". Nevertheless, much of the performance showed "good characterisation" and the finale closed with "a real flourish". Appalling weather conditions affected attendance at the final rehearsal and this could have had something to do with some of the above problems.

Ivor Setterfield conducted Brahms and Dvorak on April 27. He was a popular guest as was made clear in a comment in the printed programme that began: "The Leicester Symphony Orchestra has greatly enjoyed working with Ivor over these last few weeks." The Leicester Mercury referred to this comment in the review and stated that "this enjoyment was obvious in the results he obtained. The playing had real sparkle to it and was well disciplined, enthusiastic and exciting". His account of Dvorak's New World Symphony was "exciting and dramatic with cleanly articulated rhythms and good dynamic contrast". The accompaniment to Roger Owens' performance of the Brahms Second Piano Concerto was endowed with "authentic Brahmsian tone as well as lightness of touch". The reviewer concluded his remarks with the comment, "Ivor Setterfield proved, as did Roland Melia in November, that under the right leadership the LSO is capable of great things."

13. *Rejuvenation and Roland Melia*

After a very successful season both commercially and artistically, the orchestra had the difficult job of selecting a new conductor. All three of the above were in the running along with the six chosen at auditions. There was a hard choice to make, but after careful consideration, the decision was made to appoint Roland Melia.

As a prize winning cello scholar at the Royal Academy of Music, Roland Melia came to the LSO with a distinguished pedigree. He began his conducting studies in 1990 with David Roberts, the music director of the Ensemble Intercontemporain in Paris and then at the St Petersburg Conservatoire with the legendary Ilya Musin. He made his professional debut with the St Petersburg Philharmonic Orchestra and gave many performances with the St Petersburg Chamber Ensemble (with whom he also made recordings) and the St Petersburg Camerata. Later, he conducted the National Symphony Orchestra of Ireland, the Birmingham Royal Ballet and St John's Camerata.

As well as a new conductor, the LSO appointed a new leader to succeed Anne Hurst (formerly Gosling, later Tupling) who had given many years of loyal service. Christopher Windass stood in for a few concerts but for Melia's first appearance, it was Doreen Adnett who was in the leader's chair. An experienced and highly capable player, she first joined the LSO in 1950 and her appointment was met with approval from both players and audience as she was always a popular figure.

Melia's first concert as the orchestra's new conductor took place on Thursday November 7, 1996. The programme consisted of Hamish MacCunn's overture, The Land of the Mountain and of the Flood, Beethoven's Fourth Piano Concerto and Dvorak's Symphony No.5 in F major. It was an auspicious occasion. There was a large audience and real sense of expectation. The orchestra played well and critical opinion was favourable. The headline in the Leicester Mercury summed it up as "Bright Dawn of a New Era". The performance of Dvorak's Fifth was described as impressive with "obvious enthusiasm and confidence in the conductor's direction which produced good attack and dynamics, a well balanced sound and good ensemble". There was still work to do in the string department as moments of poor intonation demonstrated but overall there was great cause for optimism.

The standard continued to improve throughout the season. A performance of the C minor Symphony of Brahms in February 1997 produced this from the Mercury's critic: "Roland Melia drew some fine playing from all departments and the overall sound was well integrated and

Veteran violinist
leads the honours

A VETERAN violinist known as the First Lady of Leicestershire Music was today named in the New Year's Honours list.

Mrs Mary Thornley, 86, is among a wide range of city and county people awarded accolades.

Local people honoured included a Methodist minister, a prison governor and many business and community stalwarts.

Mrs Thornley, pictured, played with Leicester Symphony Orchestra for an astonishing 70 years, retiring only early this year.

She has been made a Member of the British Empire. Today Mrs Thornley said: "When I first got the official letter I thought it was a hoax or something.

"I was quite flummoxed but now I'm really pleased. It's super news."

Mrs Thornley started with the LSO when she was just 14 and was leader of the orchestra for nearly 30 years.

She still plays at home with a small group of friends.

Mrs Thornley plans to celebrate over the New Year with her daughter Mrs Olga Briggs and son-in-law Alan Briggs.

■ The roll of honour, Page 2.

Leicester Mercury's coverage of Mary Thornley's MBE award New Year 1995. Her first LSO concert was 19 April 1923 and her last 26 November 1992. She therefore played in each of the LSO's first 70 seasons.

balanced. His interpretation was consistent and carefully thought out with well chosen speeds and a real sense of the architecture of the piece".

The first concert of the 1997-98 season was dedicated to the memory of Mary Thornley who had been the longest serving member of the orchestra having completed seventy years service (over thirty of them as leader) until her retirement in 1992. It was a remarkable achievement for which she was given an MBE the following year. The concert was a fitting tribute as the Mercury pointed out. The programme consisted of Dvorak's Cello Concerto and Rachmaninov's Second Symphony. The critic began his review; "After just a year as principal conductor, I'm sure no one regrets the appointment of Roland Melia. It is clear that conductor and orchestra enjoy working together and have great rapport. The sound of the orchestra has been transformed. All sections are now extremely well balanced and far more integrated…These were well thought out interpretations notable for their clarity, rhythmic drive and richness of sound".

There was no doubt that, like his predecessors in their early years, Roland Melia had a rejuvenating effect on both the players and the audience. Concerts began to acquire a greater sense of occasion; attendance figures were improving and there was a real sense of purpose and direction among the players. Special events were arranged such as the Musical Soiree at The City Rooms in September 1997 where Melia and the members of the orchestra launched the coming season's programme with a buffet and informal concert.

The orchestra was spreading its wings. In June 1998 two concerts were planned to take it away from its city venue and out into the wider world. The first was a concert of popular classics in St George's Church, Rugby and then on Sunday June 21, a Royal British Legion Concert was held in the grounds of Beaumanor Hall at Woodhouse, near Loughborough. This was a huge success, with a fine evening and a happy picnic crowd helping to raise funds for the Royal Naval Benevolent Trust, the Army Benevolent Fund, the Royal Air Force Benevolent Fund and the 1998 Poppy Appeal. The firework finale to the accompaniment of Tchaikovsky's 1812 Overture was particularly spectacular.

Typical LSO concert programmes of the late 1990s.

The 1998-1999 season saw the orchestra expanding its activities further; this time by commissioning a new work. The composer was Walter Fabeck whose interest in electronic music had resulted in the invention of the Chromasone – an extraordinary device comprising a chrome and Perspex structure that glows in the dark. It tilts and rotates to vary the pitch and is played by a pair of "data gloves". The effect is rather eerie, but as was reported in the Leicester Mercury: "It was quite effective and fascinating to watch." Fabeck was commissioned by the orchestra to write a concerto for his new instrument and he came to Leicester to give the first performance. The complex rhythms and structures of the work "presented the orchestra with a real challenge".

Another name to appear in the programme at this concert was that of the internationally renowned oboist, Nicholas Daniel. It was announced that he had agreed to succeed Mrs Goldsmith as the orchestra's new president and that the orchestra "looked forward to his involvement and to him joining us on the platform at some future concert". With hindsight, these words have extraordinary significance.

Publicity for the Royal British Legion concert at Beaumanor Hall, June 21, 1998.

ABOVE, LEFT and BELOW: Crowds bask in the sun to enjoy the music at Beaumonaor Hall

A classical day out!

FLAG-WAVER: A concert-goer laps up the patriotic tunes

HUNDREDS of people enjoyed a special open-air concert at Beaumanor Hall near Loughborough.

A 71-piece Leicester Symphony Orchestra provided the 14-piece programme and the musical accompaniment to Quorn-born soprano soloist, Joanna Shacklock.

An audience of 1,700 people, many of whom took along their own tables and chairs and enjoyed champagne and smoked salmon picnics, entered into the spirit of the Glyndebourne-inspired occasion.

After nightfall, proceedings came to a rousing conclusion with Tchaikovsky's 1812 overture, accompanied by a spectacular firework display.

Earlier, the orchestra had provided a

Pictures: Graeme Winlow

varied programme, which ranged from Nicolai's overture to The Merry Wives of Windsor, through Grieg's beautifully-descriptive Morning from Peer Gynt, to Sibelius' sonorously-stirring Finlandia.

This was the latest in a series of consistently high-quality outdoor and indoor concerts they have organised to raise funds for the Poppy Appeal and ancillary military charities.

The beneficiaries of this one - the 1998 Poppy Appeal, the Royal Naval Benevolent Trust, the Army Benevolent Fund and the Royal Air Force Benevolent Fund - will each receive an estimated sum of at least £1,500.

FUN DAY: The music brings a smile to face of concert-goers

Leicester Mercury review of the open air concert at Beaumanor Hall.

The orchestra also ran two instrumental workshops with distinguished teachers to allow both players and members of the public to develop their musicianship and with the idea of improving the quality of the sound of the orchestra. In view of critical comment at this time to the effect that the sound the players made was both improving and much more integrated, these workshops appear to have paid off.

The first concert of 1999 saw the LSO joined by the Leicester Philharmonic Choir for a first half that consisted of popular opera choruses such as the Triumphal Scene from Aida, the Anvil Chorus and the chorus of the Hebrew Slaves. But it was the second half that showed just what the orchestra was capable of achieving under Roland Melia. Their account of Gustav Holst's orchestral showpiece The Planets, drew this from the critic of the Leicester Mercury: "The LSO was on top form… Roland Melia's conducting draws out the best from his forces and all sections played with style and confidence. The balance was good and speeds were well chosen to allow

PHOTO: COURTESY OF SARAH BROOKMAN

LSO at Beaumanor Hall with conductor Roland Melia, in the white jacket. June 21, 1998.

expressive phrasing. There was a wide dynamic range with some really powerful climaxes and each movement was strongly characterised. War, love, jollity, old age, magic and mystery were all portrayed with conviction and feeling".

The one hundred and twenty fifth anniversary of the Leicester Mercury was celebrated in a charity concert sponsored by the newspaper given in April 1999. In the summer of that year the orchestra visited Ghent in what was its first ever trip abroad. Soon after returning to England, conductor and players were back at Beaumanor at the request of the Royal British Legion for another highly successful open air firework concert.

In September 1999, a further informal musical evening was held, this time in the Civic Centre at Braunstone. A recital by the soprano, Alessandra Testai, was followed by short works performed by groups of instrumentalists from the orchestra. The event was free and like the musical soiree at The City Rooms, it helped to raise the profile of the LSO and gave the public a chance to see them perform at close range.

Another Leicester Mercury sponsored concert held on November 11, began the 1999-2000 season in style, with an evening of operatic overtures, intermezzos and arias. The guests were soprano Alessandra Testai and tenor, Geraint Dodd. This drew a large audience and numbers remained good for the February 2000 concert when the main work of the evening was Mahler's Fifth Symphony.

The LSO and the Philharmonia Orchestra joined forces for a workshop on Sunday

Publicity for the LSO Chromasone concert on November 14, 1998.

December 12, at the Leicester Adult Education College. The Philharmonia is universally acknowledged to be one of the world's finest orchestras and the management of the De Montfort Hall had been successful some two years earlier, in securing a residency for it in Leicester. This meant at least ten concerts a year with some of the world's finest artists as well as various other musical activities such as family days, educational programmes and workshops.

The Philharmonia's presence has enhanced the audience for orchestral music in the city and this has helped the LSO whose concert attendance figures had been steadily increasing since 1995. Wisely, the Council of Management at the LSO (now chaired by the orchestra's principal cellist,

Eerie show sets the night aglow!

**THE Leicester Symphony Orchestra,
De Montfort Hall
Review: Neil Crutchley**

THE LSO is playing very well these days. There's a real sense of commitment and enthusiasm, excellent phrasing and articulation, good balance, attack and integration.

There's still a little room for improvement in string intonation and tone production, but it's getting better all the time.

The concert began with a commission from the orches-

tra: The Concerto for Chromasone by Walter Fabeck. It's complex rhythms and structures presented the players with a real challenge. The chromasone is a hi-tech chrome and perspex structure which rotates and tilts to vary pitch. It also glows in the dark. It is played by flexing the fingers in a pair of data gloves. The effect is rather eerie but quite effective and it's fascinating to watch.

Mozart came next in an elegantly phrased and well-balanced performance of his 21st

Piano Concerto. The young Evgenia Chudinovitch has a brilliant yet seemingly effortless technique.

Roland Melia led the orchestra with real authority and confidence in Saint-Saens' Symphony No 3 for Organ and Orchestra with well chosen speeds and strong, incisive playing. A few moments of untidiness were a small price to pay for such an expressive performance.

The splendid De Montfort Hall organ was played by Rupert Damerell.

Leicester Mercury review of the Chromasone concert.

Pat Dobson) had taken full advantage of having a world renowned orchestra in its midst and one of the results was this workshop collaboration.

As it happened, Mahler's Fifth was the last work Roland Melia was to conduct with the Leicester Symphony Orchestra. His duties as the Principal Conductor of the Cyprus Chamber Orchestra (a post he gained in 1998) were taking more and more of his time and it was becoming almost impossible for him to return to England for long enough to take rehearsals and concerts for the LSO. In fact he was not able to take the final concert of the season. This was a pity as it was an innovative programme called "Beethoven – The Last Master" and featured the broadcaster and writer, John Suchet. It also featured

LEICESTER SYMPHONY ORCHESTRA

Gustav Holst

Thursday
11th February 1999
7.45 pm

De Montfort Hall

with the
Leicester Philharmonic
Choir
(Conductor: Richard Dacey)

Conductor: Roland Melia
Leader: Doreen Adnett

de montfort hall

NATIONAL FEDERATION
OF MUSIC SOCIETIES

Leicester
City Council

NFMS

Cover of LSO concert programme February 1999.

orchestral arrangements by Roland Melia of sections of three of Beethoven's piano sonatas.

As the author of a widely acclaimed three volume biography of Beethoven and one of the country's best known newsreaders, Suchet was a considerable draw. His programme consisted of an anecdotal account of Beethoven's life with musical illustrations and two complete performances - Egmont Overture and the Pastoral Symphony. The orchestra was rehearsed and conducted by Paul Hilliam who had, until recently, been in charge of the Charnwood Orchestra and was now Musical Director of the Heart of England Orchestra. He was also on the rostrum for the third of the summer British Legion concerts at Beaumanor Hall.

With his now full time post in Cyprus, it was impossible for Roland Melia to continue with the LSO and he resigned at the end of the 1999-2000 season. The players were sorry to see him go, as during his short time as conductor, he had had a tremendous effect both on the quality of the playing and the orchestra's prominence in the city. He had been supported in all these new ventures by Pat Dobson and the Council of Management. As a group of volunteers they do an enormous amount of work in promotion, raising funds, and general administration. The orchestra could not function without such a dedicated team and an enthusiastic and hard-working chairperson. Audiences were up, the orchestra's outlook was widened and there was a strong sense of identity. Extra activities had proved a success and musical standards both technically and artistically had seldom been higher.

14. The Path to Nicholas

There was a huge response to the orchestra's advertisement to find Melia's successor and out of a total of almost forty applicants a short list of ten was drawn up; six of whom attended auditions in May 2001. The other four had been previous guest conductors who had stepped in during Melia's absence and during the interregnum. They were Paul Hilliam, Susan Dingle, Huw Gareth Williams and Nicholas Daniel, the orchestra's recently appointed president.

Huw Gareth Williams conducted the first concert of the 2000-2001 season. He had been described on BBC Wales as "Wales' top young conducting talent" and had studied with Martyn Brabbins at the Royal Scottish Academy. As the winner of the Post Office Young Conductor's Award, he had already worked with several BBC orchestras and proved a popular guest with the LSO. His programme consisted of Copland's Fanfare for the Common Man, Beethoven's Violin Concerto and Scheherazade by Rimsky-Korsakov. The soloist was Caroline Balding. The orchestra sounded "confident and integrated" and despite some overwhelming of the soloist in the Beethoven, the performance was impressive. The conductor "really came into his own with a fine performance of Scheherazade".

Susan Dingle took the baton for the second concert which was given jointly with the Leicester Philharmonic Choir. The main work was Carl Orff's Carmina Burana. Having spent many years in opera administration, Susan Dingle began to study conducting in 1994. Since then she has conducted many British orchestras.

The concert, whilst not being one of the most memorable (it contained a rather tepid account of Richard Strauss' passionate tone poem Death and Transfiguration), was notable for another world premiere: Rachel Leach's rather pretentiously titled, The Amortisation of Intangible Fixed Assets. This turned out to be a suite of three short movements "each with a period of revelation and a period of demise" that made little impact on the audience and was described by one eminent local composer as "clever, but instantly forgettable". Susan Dingle proved to be a popular figure with the players and she scored highly in the vote for a new conductor.

Nicholas Daniel, the orchestra's president, conducted the final concert of the season and his programme began with Elgar's Cockaigne Overture. Joyce Parkin, reviewing for the Mercury felt the performance "did not work, the start was weak and there was poor ensemble". Daniel himself was the soloist in Vaughan Williams' Oboe Concerto where "the orchestra rose to the occasion in this rarely heard work". The symphony was Tchaikovsky's Fourth. Here Daniel produced some "moving moments, especially in the second movement and the pizzicato third". The concert helped to raise money for the Lord Mayor of Leicester's Macmillan appeal.

The auditions were held and orchestral members voted out of the ten candidates. Nicholas Daniel won. This is not surprising as he is a first class musician of international standing who could give a great deal to the orchestra. The fact that someone of his calibre wanted to be considered as its conductor was a compliment to the LSO. However due to Daniel's busy schedule he could not take up his post until April 2002. So two of those auditioned, Jason Thornton and Pavel Kotla, were invited to take a concert each and both turned out to be impressive musicians.

To launch the 2001-2002 season, a gala charity concert in aid of LOROS, the hospice charity for Leicestershire and Rutland, was planned. It took the title A Gala Night at the Opera and consisted of vocal and orchestral excerpts from popular operas with the soprano, Katerina Mina and the tenor, Dominic Natoli. It was a successful evening due in no small measure to the abilities and personality of the conductor, Jason Thornton. He was an excellent compere and gave the occasion a real sense of fun. His conducting was stylish and he was rewarded with fine playing.

Thornton was a popular figure but his programme was relatively lightweight, whereas Pavel Kotla who appeared in February 2002, had his work cut out with Elgar's fiendishly difficult First Symphony. He gave some idea of his abilities in a "direct and unsentimental" account of Rachmaninov's Second Piano Concerto with Charles Owen as soloist. But the Elgar had something extra. It was a "polished and

LEICESTER MERCURY **23**

Orchestra really rose to the occasion

Leicester Symphony Orchestra
De Montfort Hall
Review: Joyce Parkin

LEICESTER Symphony Orchestra gave a concert conducted by Nicholas Daniel, who was also soloist in Vaughan Williams' Oboe Concerto.

The orchestra rose to the occasion in this rarely-heard work.

This pastoral piece, with three short movements, has melodious themes and intricate rhythms and makes for very pleasant listening. It was well executed by Nicholas Daniel. There was lovely conversation between strings and soloist.

The concert began with Elgar's Cockaigne Overture, which depicts all aspects of life "In London Town" – street urchins, lovers in the park.

Unfortunately, for me, this performance did not work. The start was weak, there was poor ensemble, meaning that the playing lacked definition.

However, things were different in Tchaikovsky's best-loved Symphony, No 4 in F minor.

Under Daniel's baton, we heard moving moments, especially in the second movement and in the pizzicato third.

■ The concert was in aid of the Lord Mayor's Macmillan Appeal Fund and was sponsored by the Leicester Mercury.

Leicester Mercury review of Nicholas Daniel's first LSO concert, May 2001.

Nicholas Daniel in rehearsal with violinist Min Jin in April 2002.

LSO hard at work in rehearsal in April 2002.

lyrical performance" with "strong forward impetus, brisk speeds and moments of melting lyricism". Kotla drew "fine playing from all departments, with well built, resonant climaxes and good rhythmic definition".

Nicholas Daniel's first concert in his new post was on April 25, 2002 and his programme contained Berlioz's Roman Carnival Overture, Sibelius' Violin Concerto with Min Jin as soloist, Dvorak's Eighth Slavonic Dance and the Third Symphony by Brahms. There was a good house and a strong sense of expectation. The Berlioz opened the concert in style. It was a performance of "great vitality and momentum with tremendous forward drive and well built climaxes". Min Jin's Sibelius had "considerable stature" and the orchestra "had rarely played with more dynamism and panache than it did in Dvorak's Slavonic Dance No.8. The whip-crack attack and sense of abandon were very impressive". The Brahms was given an effective performance with "the conductor's desire to push forward emphasising the heroic rather than the reflective, autumnal qualities of the work and probably accounting for the odd woolly passage". Overall, the concert was very well received with the Leicester Mercury's headline stating that, "This Could Be The Start Of A Beautiful Musical Friendship."

In June 2002 the orchestra made another trip overseas. This time it was to celebrate the Queen's Golden Jubilee and mark the beginning of the LSO's eightieth birthday celebrations. Strasbourg, one of Leicester's twin cities, was the destination and two concerts were given in the first three days of the month. The programmes included works from the previous Leicester concert with Elgar's Cockaigne Overture and Imperial March, Humperdinck's Hansel and Gretel Overture, Brahms' Third Symphony and an Adagio for Cor Anglais and Strings by Mozart (with

De Montfort Hall concert, conductor Nicholas Daniel and violinist Min Jin, April 25, 2002

Nicholas Daniel as soloist) thrown in for good measure.

By all accounts, the orchestra not only acquitted itself with distinction, its members had a hugely enjoyable time with plenty of opportunities for sightseeing and wine tasting. There were a few anxious moments such as the conductor missing his train (but not the concert) and one of the players developing a painful leg problem that required a trip to hospital for tests. Nonetheless, it was a very successful trip and a good start to the anniversary year.

Preceding her departure from Leicester to London in the spring of 2002, Mrs Ruth Goldsmith resigned as president of the orchestra. She had served in this capacity since the death in 1983 of her husband, Dr Mac Goldsmith, and continued to offer the very practical help and support he had given. She was an active president who rarely missed a concert and was very adept at persuading her friends and associates to support the orchestra either as patrons or by donating to the funds. She retained her connection with the LSO as one of its vice presidents, but had been succeeded briefly as president by Nicholas Daniel. However, with his appointment as conductor, the search was on again.

It wasn't long before an announcement was made. The orchestra's new president was the internationally known composer and broadcaster Michael Berkeley, whose father Sir Lennox Berkeley, was one of the leading composers of the generation of Tippett and Britten. Having artistic association with such well-known musical figures as Nicholas Daniel and Michael Berkeley would be sure to raise the LSO's profile as it entered its ninth decade.

Three concerts were planned for the orchestra's eightieth birthday celebration season. The first, on November 14, attracted a large audience and included a fine performance of Sibelius' Second Symphony as well as an affectionate account of Mozart's Clarinet Concerto from Joy Farrell. This concert was repeated at Dudley Town Hall on Saturday November 16, as a charity concert for the RNLI.

Cellist Guy Johnston, a winner of the BBC Young Musician competition, and his violinist brother Magnus, were the guests at the concert on February 8, 2003. They were the soloists in an impressive performance of Brahms' Double Concerto that was both searching and dynamic.

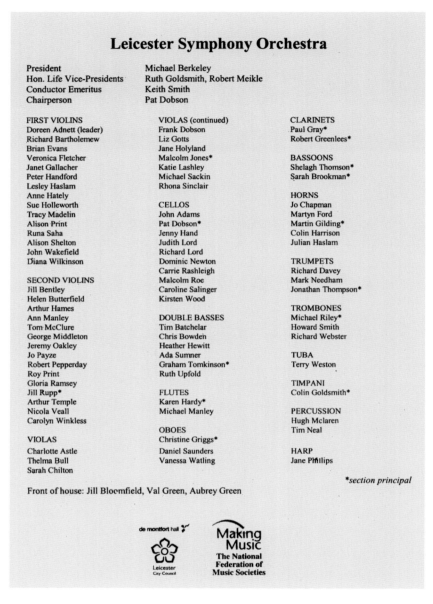

LSO player list of November 2002.

This was followed by a powerful reading of Tchaikovsky's Fifth Symphony in which Daniel once again showed his distinctive and persuasive musical personality.

The final concert in the eightieth birthday season was, appropriately enough, a joint presentation with the Leicester Philharmonic Choir which, in turn, was augmented by the Charnwood Choral Society and the Countesthorpe Community College Choir. The work chosen was Elgar's oratorio, The Dream of Gerontius. This was an apt choice as it was one of the works Sargent conducted in the De Montfort Hall in early 1922 with the pilot orchestra from which the LSO was formed.

This concert was a great success and provided a splendid finale to the anniversary season. It was an occasion that recalled the glory days of pre-war LSO concerts with the Philharmonic Choir under Sargent's mesmerising baton. There was a large audience and a tremendous atmosphere in the hall. Nicholas Daniel spoke of the great privilege of conducting a work like Gerontius and then proceeded to direct a searing, passionate performance that by common consent reached the heart of the piece in a way that was quite remarkable. The Leicester Mercury stated that it "blazed with conviction" and that "choirs, orchestra and soloists responded to the conductor's fervent direction with enthusiasm and dedication". It went on to say that the

LEICESTER SYMPHONY ORCHESTRA

Thursday

22nd May 2003

7.45pm

De Montfort Hall

Conductor:	Nicholas Daniel
Leader:	Doreen Adnett
Oboe:	Nicholas Daniel
Mezzo Soprano:	Catherine King
Tenor:	Charles Daniels
Bass:	Brindley Sherratt

Cover of LSO concert programme, May 2003. This concert with Leicester Philharmonic Choir, featuring Elgar's Dream of Gerontius, won the Leicester Mercury's The Week award for the best classical performance of 2003. For Nicholas Daniel, this was his most memorable concert with LSO.

performance "wasn't without its rough edges, but these mattered little in an account that captured the spirit of the work so effectively … the singing had both great power and exquisite delicacy. Tenor, Charles Daniels was an impressively passionate and intense Gerontius, mezzo, Catherine King, a radiant, golden-toned angel and bass, Brindley Sherratt brought power and authority to his joint roles of Priest and Angel of the Agony".

After the concert, there was a noticeable buzz of excitement and optimism in the foyer of the De Montfort Hall as everyone knew they had experienced something special. To crown the celebration season this concert received the Leicester Mercury award for the Best Classical Performance of the Year, presented at the awards ceremony held in the De Montfort Hall in January 2004.

Daniel's success continued into the 2003-2004 season and for the first concert, on November 13, 2003, he managed to secure the services of the outstanding Australian pianist Piers Lane, who gave a powerful account of Schumann's Piano Concerto. The concert began with a rarity – at least for Leicester: the King Lear Overture by Berlioz – and it ended with a work that on its first appearance, caused both controversy and admiration: Anthony Payne's "realisation" of the sketches of Elgar's Symphony No.3. The story behind the work is a complicated one.

Elgar had died before completing the symphony which had been commissioned, at a fee of £1,000, by the BBC. There had been speculation about the extent of the work done at the time of his death, but the dying composer had been quite clear that he didn't want anything done to the sketches. In fact, he asked his close friend, the violinist W H Reed to burn the manuscript with the comment: "It's all bits and pieces...Don't let anyone tinker with it...they wouldn't understand."

Reed didn't burn the sketches and they were published as a facsimile in the back of his biography of Elgar. However in 1993 Anthony Payne was asked by Paul Hindmarsh of the BBC to put the sketches into "some sort of shape for a workshop performance". Payne jumped at the chance and remarked: "These pages contain the vestiges of an inspired work, yet they seem to have aroused little interest until comparatively recently." After this promising start, the project was abandoned as the Elgar family felt honour bound to respect the composer's dying wishes. But after an illustrated broadcast on the sketches given by Dr Payne in March 1995, and the realisation that it was possible for him to complete the work, permission was given and the Elgar family commissioned a completed version of the symphony; which was just as well, because by 2005 the sketches would be out of copyright and that meant that anyone would be able to "tinker" with them.

The result more than justified the family's decision, and Daniel's passionate and assured performance with the LSO was one of the first by a non-professional orchestra. It was warmly received and showed that the conductor had both the courage to programme a work that would need to be carefully prepared from scratch (very few people had heard the piece at this point) and the personality to bring it off. Once again the comparison with Sargent looms large.

The season continued with a performance of Mahler's Symphony No. 1 in February 2004, that was described by the Leicester Mercury critic as "extremely well integrated and balanced". He described Daniel's conducting as "highly expressive" and had this to say about the orchestra in general: "The last decade has seen a great change in the Leicester Symphony Orchestra. It was always a competent local ensemble...Now thanks to Nicholas Daniel and his predecessor Roland Melia, it is an ensemble of real distinction that plays with passion and enthusiasm." This concert began with Gregorian Variations for Orchestra by the the orchestra's president, Michael Berkeley. This is a colourful single movement work in four sections based on Gregorian chant but also using jazz and pop elements. Berkeley was present for the performance, prior to which he had been interviewed by Neil Roberts in an entertaining pre-concert talk.

The final concert of the season marked the retirement of two of the LSO's longest serving members: Doreen Adnett the orchestra's leader for the past eight seasons and Martin Gilding, principal horn since 1978. Between them, these two players had clocked up ninety five years of service; Doreen Adnett had been in the LSO for 54 years and had played under five different conductors and Martin Gilding, who was also a long-serving member of the orchestra's Council of Management, joined as third horn in 1963.

PHOTO: COURTESY OF SARAH BROOKMAN

Doreen Adnett, member of LSO for 60 years and leader from 1996 to 2004.

The concert itself drew "a considerably smaller audience than the LSO has enjoyed of late", the Leicester Mercury critic observed. This was probably due to the choice of the main work: Bruckner's Fourth Symphony; the effect of which wasn't alleviated by also including Rossini's sparkling overture to the Italian Girl in Algiers and Mozart's Fourth Horn Concerto with Stephen Bell as soloist. Of the symphony, the critic had this to say: "Conductor and orchestra put their heart and soul into the Bruckner and produced an impressive sound for this heavyweight work, which stretched the players to their limits – and just occasionally, beyond. They gave every ounce to ensure Daniel's powerful and atmospheric interpretation came across with conviction."

The Bruckner symphony was the work the orchestra performed on their Paris tour at the end of May 2004. It was prefaced by the short but exquisite Ave Verum Corpus by Mozart. Fifty two members of the LSO along with spouses, parents and friends travelled in two coaches to the French capital where they stayed in an hotel close to the Eiffel Tower. Two concerts were given, both under Nicholas Daniel and guest leader Jane Sinclair, and they both "went well". The first was in the church of St Roche near the Louvre and the second in the American Cathedral, close to the Champs Elysees. The concert in St Roche attracted a packed house with standing room only". The retiring collection raised £500. The cathedral concert attracted a smaller audience but several of those who did attend described the orchestra's performance as "magnificent". Mike Lord, commenting on the tour, said the resonant acoustic of the building gave the orchestra "a tremendous sound".

A new leader appeared on the De Montfort Hall stage for the November 11 concert. He was Mike Shaw, who had studied at the Birmingham Conservatoire and led both orchestras there. An experienced player and soloist, Shaw had worked with many orchestras in England and Europe. He had been teaching violin and viola for Arts in Education in Leicestershire and was currently conductor of both its junior strings ensemble and the Nottingham Youth Training Orchestra.

Shaw's first appearance with the LSO was in a programme that included three works by Tchaikovsky: Nutcracker Suite, Rococo Variations and Andante Cantabile, along with Dvorak's 8th Symphony. The solo cellist was the internationally acclaimed Natalie Clein, - another example of Nicholas Daniel's desire to have the best for the orchestra. The performance of the Rococo Variations was "beautifully realised, with strong, yet poetic playing" from Natalie Clein, who was admirably supported by the orchestra. The Andante Cantabile was "exquisite in its delicacy and feeling".

It was no surprise that this concert drew a large audience, and although "intonation and ensemble were not at their best" at the beginning of the Nutcracker Suite, things quickly improved and each movement of Dvorak's 8th was "lovingly characterised and phrased". The review of this concert ended with this observation:

"Nicholas Daniel has strong interpretative ideas and his flexible approach to speed means that his players have to be alert. In general, they are, although the sudden (and risky) acceleration in the closing bars of the symphony nearly caught them out."

Graham Oppenheimer, a well-known Leicester-born viola player and founder of the Leicester International Music Festival, was the soloist in a performance of Berlioz's Harold in Italy for the February 2005 concert. This was the final part of a demanding programme that also included the Four Sea Interludes from Peter Grimes by Benjamin Britten and "a real test for the orchestra", Copland's Four Dance Episodes from Rodeo. All the pieces were successfully realised with critic Stephen Gamble stating that Daniel "added the necessary rhythmic lilt to the American folk tunes" in Rodeo, which was enhanced by the "outstanding" percussion section.

There was an extra concert in the 2004-2005 season in the form of another of the LSO's occasional collaborations with the Leicester Philharmonic Choir. This time the work in question was the rarely heard oratorio Christus by Franz Liszt. This enormous work requires, not only orchestra and choir, but also five soloists, narrator and organ. A distinguished line-up of soloists was engaged, headed by the celebrated actor Simon Callow as narrator. The conductor was the concert pianist and Liszt expert, Leslie Howard. The successful performance, promoted by the Liszt Society, attracted a reasonable audience and received an enthusiastic review.

Twelve days after the Liszt came the last of the season's concerts and this time it was directed by guest conductor Russell Keable and included Knussen's Flourish with Fireworks, Ravel's Mother Goose Suite and Bolero. The magnificently restored De Montfort Hall organ, played by Richard Archer, was in action for the final work, the Symphony No. 3 in C minor by Saint-Saens.

15. The Search for a Successor

The pressures of an international career as an oboe soloist, a new professorship in Germany and intense study with world renowned conductors Mariss Jansons and Sir Simon Rattle, meant that sooner or later Nicholas Daniel was going to have to give up his post with the Leicester Symphony Orchestra, and this happened in the period prior to the 2005-2006 season. His time in charge had been a highlight of the orchestra's eighty three years.

Pat Dobson, the LSO's long-standing chairperson said: "I cannot overemphasise the effect he has had on the orchestra. Nick has the rare quality of being able to combine great musicality, huge enthusiasm and excellent communication skills to make playing for him such a great pleasure. He is the sort of person who makes everyone want to do their very best and this is well reflected in the considerable improvement in playing within the orchestra over his time with us. He is leaving us to further his career and we consider ourselves very fortunate indeed to have had Nick as our conductor over the past few years."

The feeling was mutual. Daniel said it was "painful to leave my friends in the LSO" and wrote: "I have found audiences and musicians to be wonderfully warm and open, honest too (to a fault occasionally!!) but always respectful of my love for music and deeply supportive. Two of the performances I shall never in my life forget, were our Brahms 3 in Strasbourg and our Bruckner 4 in Paris in the huge American Cathedral. The way both those concerts felt, was as though we were in any great hall from Symphony Hall to Carnegie Hall, performing at the highest level, not perhaps in terms of accuracy, but in terms of musical intensity and communication we found together on those occasions, and on many since. A real highlight of our performances together in Leicester was our award winning performance of Elgar's Dream of Gerontius. It's a transcending masterpiece on many levels and that performance really changed things for me."

Daniel concluded his comments with a typical flourish: "Thank you for coming to our concerts, dear audience, how marvellous to see you in growing numbers all the time, and thank you LSO for teaching me so much and for believing in and trusting me."

Inevitably there were occasional dissenting voices during Daniel's reign, largely due to his ambition to perform expensive works and his desire to have the best available soloists which, of course, are not cheap. But the same criticism was made during Malcolm Sargent's time and happily neither conductor allowed himself to be influenced by such reservations. And no-one

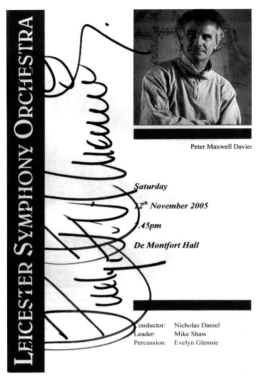

Peter Maxwell Davies

Saturday

12th November 2005

7.45pm

De Montfort Hall

Conductor: Nicholas Daniel
Leader: Mike Shaw
Percussion: Evelyn Glennie

*Autographed cover of Evelyn Glennie concert,
November 2005 – a complete sell-out.*

could deny that, like Sargent's, Daniel's time with the LSO brought enormous benefits.

Daniel's last concert, took place on Saturday November 12, 2005. The programme consisted of nine items including Vivaldi's Piccolo Concerto No.11 in C major, Arthur Thornley's arrangement of Bach's Toccata and Fugue in D minor, Tchaikovsky's 1812 Overture, Sibelius's Karelia Suite and the Orkney Wedding and Sunrise by Sir Peter Maxwell Davies. The piccolo concerto was played in an arrangement for vibraphone made by the evening's soloist, the renowned Evelyn Glennie, who was also the soloist in Askell Masson's Concerto for Snare Drum and Orchestra and the bagpiper in the Maxwell Davies.

The headline of the Leicester Mercury review read: "Music lets the sunshine pour in". Stephen Gamble enjoyed the Snare Drum Concerto but was less enthusiastic about the Vivaldi transcription, stating that the vibraphone "sounds like a door chime". The orchestra's best performances came in Saint-Saens' Danse Macabre, "where Mike Shaw took Death's part with disconcerting ease, and in the Orkney Wedding with appropriately inebriated trombones and boozy violas". LSO records show a sell out attendance just short of 1,500, certainly their biggest audience since the Diamond Jubilee, Julian Lloyd Webber concert in November 1982.

In the printed programme to this concert Pat Dobson wrote:

"Over the last few months we have been busy looking for a new conductor to take over from Nick. I am very pleased to announce that we have appointed Pavel Kotla, who will be taking up his position with us next April. Pavel was a guest conductor with us in February 2002 in Rachmaninov Piano Concerto No.2 and Elgar's Symphony No.1, which were particularly well received. We are very much looking forward to working again with Pavel."

Pavel Kotla was born in Poland and studied at the Chopin Academy of Music in Warsaw. He received his graduate degree in performance practice and musicology with Andrew Parrott of the Taverner Choir and Players and Edward Higginbottom of New College, Oxford. Between 1998 and 2003 he was a regular assistant conductor to Sir Simon Rattle and worked on such projects as Towards the Millennium and Hear Now festivals. Kotla had worked with several professional ensembles in the UK and internationally and brought an impressive range of experience to his work with the LSO.

There was one concert to go before Kotla took up his post and this was a significant one as it was the first of a series of successful collaborations with the comedian and musician Rainer Hersch. It was fortunate that the LSO's second concert invariably coincided with Leicester's increasingly popular comedy festival. A wise Council of Management saw an opportunity to gain a new audience and to do something different.

Hersch has performed on every major comedy stage in Britain and abroad. He has been hailed as a successor to the late Victor Borge. He took up a career in musical management but soon realised that his true vocation was in comedy. He began with cabaret and stand-up events, but soon combined his two great loves, which originally manifested itself in All Classical Music Explained, the first of several music-comedy presentations. He is now a well established entertainer, popular with audiences not only through his live appearances but also his journalism, TV and radio work.

Hersch's first LSO concert took place on 17 February 2006 and was in fact "All Classical Music Explained. "The programme was designed to answer questions such as "What does the conductor actually do?" and "What are they actually singing about in opera?" The music included Rossini's William Tell Overture, Beethoven's Emperor Concerto, Gershwin's Summertime, Pachelbel's Canon, Leroy Anderson's Sleigh Ride and Strauss's Radetzky March. The event was a great success and drew a large audience, many of whom were hearing the LSO for the first time.

The orchestra repeated the concert later that year on Sunday July 16, at Walpole Park, Ealing, where they played in a marquee under a blazing sun and a temperature of "95 degrees in the shade". The publicity for this concert included a quotation from The Scotsman which read: "Even if you can't tell a string quartet from a string vest, this show is a guaranteed laugh." The items played included "Beethoven's 'da da da daaa' Symphony" (No.5), a concerto for typewriter and "that song off the British Airways advert" (Flower Duet from Lakme).

Pavel Kotla's first concert as the LSO's new conductor, on May 29, 2006, didn't take place in Leicester, but on the orchestra's fourth overseas tour. This time the destination was northern Germany and

Pavel Kotla who conducted the LSO from May 2006 until June 2009.

included Aachen and Leicester's twin city of Krefeld. Here the orchestra was given a civic welcome and a reception hosted by the Mayor of Krefeld.

Violinist Tom McClure described the evening's concert, which was sold out and attended by an appreciative audience, including Mayor Gregor Kathstede: "The orchestra started well, supported by two local professional double bass players, and marked performances by our brass and woodwind sections.

"With the audience warming to our performances of Weber's Overture to Oberon, Borodin's In the Steppes of Central Asia, and Elgar's Three Bavarian Dances, we paused for the interval and returned for a thrilling rendition of Tchaikovsky's 6th Symphony. This was evident particularly from the spontaneous applause and shouts of "bravo!" after the rousing third movement....As an encore we had prepared Elgar's Nimrod and our audience welcomed the opportunity to applaud once more."

"The second concert took place in Aachen. It was less formal than the Krefeld event and although it was not well attended, the enthusiasm of the audience resulted in an encore performance of Nimrod."

Back in Leicester on June 6, Pavel Kotla conducted Weber's Oberon Overture, Rachmaninov's Rhapsody on a Theme of Paganini with Min-Jung Kym as soloist and Tchaikovsky's 6th Symphony. The programme included a paragraph headed: "Welcome to Pavel" and began: "The Leicester Symphony Orchestra is delighted to welcome Pavel Kotla as our newly appointed Musical Director. Over seventy-five candidates applied for this post and Pavel was the overwhelming favourite choice of the LSO."

The orchestra's first appearance of the new season was something out of the ordinary at the Abbey Park Bonfire and Firework Display on November 4, when Darth Vader put in a menacing appearance. A fortnight later the players were back on the familiar ground of the De Montfort Hall for A Night at the Movies. This event attracted a large audience and also an enthusiastic review from Peter Collett, a new member of the Leicester Mercury reviewing team, who

PHOTO: COURTESY OF LEICESTER MERCURY

Darth Vader stands menacingly as Pavel Kotla conducts the bonfire night concert at Abbey Park in November 2006. It was a very cold night!

REVIEWS

Music from movies moved me

THERE is much music written today to be used as themes or background music to films, while other music written long before cinema was thought of has come to greater public attention because it has been used in the movies.

In either case, it is easy to forget that much of this is fine music in its own right.

In their first concert of the season, the Leicester Symphony Orchestra gave us the opportunity to enjoy 12 pieces of music from numerous box-office hits.

The challenge of the concert

Leicester Symphony Orchestra; Conductor – Pavel Kotla.

De Montfort Hall, Leicester

Review by Peter Collett

was to convey many different musical moods: from the drama of The Lord of the Rings: The Fellowship of the Ring Symphonic Suite, to the emotion of the Theme from Schindler's List, through the mystery and magic of the Harry Potter Symphonic Suite, to the power of the Dances With Wolves Concert Suite.

The orchestra, under new con-

ductor Pavel Kotla, conveyed these moods effortlessly.

Soloists Christine Griggs (oboe) and Mike Shaw (violin) gave emotional performances in Gabriel's Oboe and Schindler's List respectively.

In the Lord of the Rings, treble soloist and Leicester Cathedral head chorister, Jack Thompson provided a tranquil interlude to the drama of the opening piece.

Concluding with the Main Title from Star Wars and an encore of the same, the Leicester Symphony Orchestra gave a quality evening of musical entertainment.

Leicester Mercury review of A Night at the Movies in November 2006.

summed up the concert as, "A quality evening of musical entertainment". He went on to say: "The challenge of the concert was to convey many different musical moods: from the drama of The Lord of the Rings: The Fellowship of the Ring Symphonic Suite, to the emotion of the theme from Schindler's List, through the mystery and magic of the Harry Potter Symphonic Suite, to the power of the Dances with Wolves Concert Suite. The orchestra, under new conductor Pavel Kotla, conveyed these moods effortlessly."

Shostakovich's Tenth Symphony was the main work in the concert of March 3, 2007. This weighty piece was programmed alongside Wagner's rarely-heard Rienzi Overture and Rodrigo's ever-popular Concierto de Aranjuez with Gary Ryan as guitar soloist.

Pavel Kotla was unable to conduct this concert and his place was taken by John Andrews, the LSO's present conductor. He made a good impression on Peter Collett whose review included these words: "The Shostakovich Symphony No. 10 in E minor contains passages of terror, torment, tranquillity and beauty. This was not an easy piece for the listener and I'm sure the same applies for the performers. However, the orchestra gave a fine rendition, conveying the different moods with authority... a sure-footed and skilful performance which was a pleasure to listen to."

Kotla was back on the De Montfort Hall rostrum for the concert on June 9, comprising Elgar's Violin Concerto and the Symphony No.4 in E minor by Brahms. Peter Collett reported that Elgar's concerto, played by Katherine Gowers, "brought emotion in bundles". However, it was the Brahms symphony that really impressed the reviewer. He wrote: "The orchestra excelled themselves...Once again the wonderful brass section was in evidence and, in the third movement in particular, lush strings and clear woodwind conveyed the melodies and themes with clarity and confidence."

Pavel Kotla was settling in to his new role with impressive authority. His performances were objective, clear and dynamic and the quality of the playing was drawing praise from many quarters. Although generally popular, Kotla's rehearsal style wasn't to everyone's taste. One long standing player, when asked if he liked the new conductor replied, "Can't say I do – he's very offhand", but even he was obliged to add, "That said, there's no denying that he gets the results – and we can certainly follow him." In contrast to this view, another player remarked. "He is a real gentleman, courteous and charming, but he insists on high standards and some people don't always like that!"

The performance of Holst's orchestral suite The Planets, which ended the first concert of the 2007-2008 season, was given in conjunction with Leicester's renowned National Space Centre and the pre-concert talk was presented by Professor Martin Barstow, Head of Physics and Astronomy at the University of Leicester. The concert began with Ingoma by Hendryk Hofmyr. The composer described his work as being "a free adaptation of Xhosa traditional music". The work uses a vast percussion section including drums, tam-tam, triangle, wood blocks and tambourine.

Catherine Turnell, reviewing for the Leicester Mercury didn't mention Ignoma and said very little about Weber's 2nd Clarinet Concerto, other than it was played with "consummate skill" by Sarah Williamson. She was saving her words for the main work of the evening and the following is a little of what she said:

"The Planets is an orchestral suite which raises goose bumps left, right and centre and Leicester Symphony Orchestra's performance of Gustav Holst's masterpiece did not fail to meet such giddy expectation on Saturday. The 80-strong ensemble, led by the tireless agility of conductor Pavel Kotla, blasted their way through the seven-movement galaxy with a gusto and panache that would have done its creator proud."

Rainer Hersch was back for the February 2008 with At Last the 1977 New Year's Day Concert, which took place on the 16th as part of the Leicester Comedy Festival. Peter Collett enjoyed the evening and it is worth reproducing at length what he had to say as it gives a flavour of a Hersch presentation. He wrote: "The concert itself lasted about 60 seconds, including presentation and applause, while the encore, complete with interval lasted for just over two hours.

"This was certainly not a concert for anyone who had come to hear classical music played in orthodox style. Comedian and musician Rainer Hersch provided comedy through his musical knowledge and experience, engaging both the audience and orchestra in his antics. Alongside well known music by Strauss, Smetana and Tchaikovsky, we heard such pieces as the Windows Waltz, based on themes that all users of computer software have been annoyed by! Opera singer

Susan Gilmour Bailey sang and gargled the Laughing Song from Die Fledermaus, complete with a hilarious phonetic translation.

"Education was provided in the form of a hilarious tour of the orchestra and an attempt to answer the question: What do conductors actually do? This was partially answered by conducting the Strauss Pizzicato Polka with juggling balls!"

The orchestra also came in for its share of praise: "The LSO looked to be the perfect comedy partner and had clearly worked hard at the complicated musical routines and comic timings. Their versatility and musicianship shone through their unusual orchestrations."

Collett described the event as: "A superb show which brought classical music down to earth, without ridicule."

The Leicester season ended with more Brahms (Academic Festival Overture) and Elgar (Enigma Variations), in between which came a "superb" account of Mendelssohn's Violin Concerto by Charlie Siem – one of today's finest young violinists.

Another trip abroad, in May, saw the LSO taking Elgar's Enigma Variations, Brahms' Academic Festival Overture, Grieg's Peer Gynt suite No.1 and Sibelius's Finlandia to Kotla's native Poland and the Czech Republic.

PHOTO: COURTESY OF JOHN HOLLINS

May 2008 - LSO and followers on steps of Wroclaw (formerly Breslau) University, where Brahms was awarded his honorary doctorate.

PHOTO: COURTESY OF SAM DOBSON

*Publicity for Jablonec concert,
29 May 2008.*

The tour included time for sightseeing and a visit to Wroclaw (formerly Breslau) University, which had a special significance for members of the LSO as, in 1876, the university conferred an honorary doctorate on Johannes Brahms and in return the composer wrote his Academic Festival Overture as a thank you gesture. The overture was one of the items the orchestra was to play on its tour.

The first concert took place in the Town Theatre in Kudowa Zdroj and LSO violinist Jeremy Oakley recalled that "a select but appreciative audience" rewarded the orchestra with a standing ovation.

Prague was the next stop and, after more sightseeing the players travelled to Jablonec and Nisou for the second concert, which was better attended and just as enthusiastically received by the audience. A standing ovation led to two encores.

By the end of 2008, it was clear that Kotla was maintaining a good standard of playing and the Leicester Mercury's review of the concert on November 15 is worth reproducing at length as a snapshot of the orchestra's qualities at that time. It begins:

"Over the past decade the Leicester Symphony Orchestra has been transformed. There is a much richer string tone, the brass is integrated and balanced and the woodwind polished and tempered. Conductor Pavel Kotla has built on his predecessors' achievements and continues to refine the sound.

"Kotla conducts with authority and confidence and his interpretation of Rachmaninov's Second Symphony that concluded this concert showed a strong musical personality. It was urgent, passionate and sensitively phrased. The relatively brisk tempi ensured a good line and a welcome lack of sentimentality. Climaxes were well-graded and sustained, string tone glowed and Paul Gray unfolded the Adagio's gorgeous clarinet solo with aplomb.

"Rimsky-Korsakov's colourful Capriccio Espagnole was also stylishly done with good dynamic contrasts, clean lines, strong rhythms and a percussion section that played with more confidence that in the symphony."

However, the conductor's reading of the opening work did not impress, and the reviewer's concluding paragraph reads:

"In contrast, Vaughan Williams's magnificent Tallis Fantasia was given a disappointingly featureless performance. Kotla's constant urging onwards seemed to flatten out the climaxes and led to a lack of clarity and moments of scrappy ensemble and intonation in a work that

PHOTO: COURTESY OF JOHN HOLLINS

Enthusiastic applause in Jablonec theatre, with conductor Pavel Kotla and leader Mike Shaw.

should glow with mystery and grandeur."

The twenty-first century has seen a widening of the LSO's activities on a scale that would have been hard to imagine in the 1960s and 70s, when the three celebrity concerts in the De Montfort Hall were the mainstay of its music making. During those years a much reduced band occasionally appeared at the Little Theatre to accompany a local opera group; but that, and one or two schools' carol concerts, is about the sum total of its activities.

By the end of the first decade of the new century, the orchestra was making regular trips abroad (something Keith Smith always hoped to do) and playing for civic occasions, such as the annual fireworks party at Abbey Park. There were also more unusual and eye catching programmes, often with a special theme. These events attract a different type of audience and widen the orchestra's appeal. Concerts are now preceded by interesting talks with guest soloists or conductors and these are ably hosted by the genial and well-informed Neil Roberts. The LSO also has an extensive website and a Facebook page.

Another themed concert took place on Saturday February 14, 2009, when the orchestra's former conductor Roland Melia returned to direct "Aspects of Love, a Valentine's Day celebration that included operatic arias and duets, art songs and extracts from popular musicals – all on the theme of love. The soloists were Katerina Mina, soprano, and James Edwards, tenor. Clare Hammond was the pianist and the concert also featured the Welsh poet Richard Douglas Pennant.

The orchestra enjoyed renewing its acquaintance with Melia. One player said: "It was nice to see Roland again. He did a lot for us at a time when we needed a boost. He drew us together and gave us a sense of esprit de corps. I enjoyed working with him; he was always good to play

PHOTO: COURTESY OF PAUL COLE

Catherine Cole (nee Axcell), joined LSO in November 2007 and was leader from June 2009.

for, easy to follow and patient in rehearsal. But he insisted on good standards and balance."

Sadly, this was the last concert with Mike Shaw as leader. He had held the post since November 2004. He was a very modest and extremely accomplished musician, who had done a huge amount to improve the orchestra's standard of play.

One of the crowning glories of classical music, Beethoven's 9th Symphony, was the concluding work in the orchestra's final concert of the 2008-2009 season, which took place on June 6, 2009. It was thirty years since Beethoven's 9th had last been performed by the LSO, then under Keith Smith. As in 1979, the orchestra was joined by the Leicester Philharmonic Choir and a distinguished group of soloists including the hugely popular television choirmaster and tenor, Gareth Malone. There was also a guest leader, Catherine Cole (nee Axcell). Catherine joined the orchestra for the November 2007 concert. She had experience of leading several orchestras in Cheshire, and Oxford – where she obtained a mathematics degree – and Surrey.

This concert, which also included Borodin's Prince Igor overture, Finlandia by Sibelius and Bajka (Fairytale) by the Polish composer Moniusko, was to be the last with Pavel Kotla as conductor. It was a fitting farewell to a brief but successful period. He had been in charge for three seasons and had taken the orchestra on two significant European tours and maintained the high standard set by predecessors. The note in the programme stated that during his time "the orchestra's repertoire and reputation has continued to grow" and concluded by saying: "The orchestra would like to thank Pavel for the significant and distinguished contribution he has made over the past three years and wish him the very best for the future."

This year saw the death of Doreen Adnett, a former leader of the LSO and a member for sixty years. She was an able and respected player who belonged to most of the local instrumental ensembles including the Bardi and Oadby and Wigston Civic orchestras. She also led the University of Leicester Sinfonia for thirty two years and was often to be seen in the pit of the Little Theatre. A tribute in the LSO programme concluded with these words: "Doreen was a much-loved member of the Leicestershire musical community and will be sadly missed by all of us in the Leicester Symphony Orchestra." The first concert of the new season was dedicated to both Doreen Adnett and long-serving member of the 2nd violins, Robert Pepperday, whose sudden death after forty years of playing in the LSO, came as a great shock to its members.

16. Who Next?

It was decided not to rush into the appointment of a new conductor. The Council of Management decided to draw up a shortlist of possioble conductors from those that were known to them or that had been recommended. The next two seasons therefore, saw a number of different personalities at the helm of the LSO, beginning on November 14, 2009 with Jason Lai who conducted the Prelude and Liebestod from Wagner's Tristan and Isolde, the Sibelius Violin Concerto with David Chivers and Shostakovich's Fifth Symphony.

The orchestra enjoyed working with Lai, but press response was rather more muted. The Leicester Mercury critic had this to say: "After a rather insipid realisation of the long opening theme, conductor Jason Lai was effective in maintaining the work's momentum and in phrasing Shostakovich's angular melodies. With precise direction, he secured some decent playing, especially from the brass and succeeded in capturing much of the work's ambivalence, despite a feeling of emotional detachment and an occasional lack of abandon in the big moments."

The old practice of beginning concerts with the National Anthem gave the orchestra an opportunity to warm up by playing something familiar, and now this is no longer done, the players have to begin the first piece without any chance to get into their stride and this isn't always successful as the critic of this concert observed:

"With its exposed string opening, it was a risk to begin the concert with the Prelude and Liebstod from Wagner's Tristan and Isolde. The playing needs to be spot-on, as it sets the scene for what follows, and unfortunately, intonation and pitch were not at their best here. The Prelude didn't really blossom, but the Liebestod gained in momentum to reach a glowing climax."

Lai was to have conducted the next concert on February 13, 2010, but dropped out and at short notice, his place was taken by Gerry Cornelius, who began with Beethoven's Coriolan Overture . Then came Brahms's 2nd Piano Concerto with soloist Charles Owen who had gained a worldwide reputation since his last appearance with LSO, and Tchaikovsky's 6th Symphony.

The highlight of the season was, without doubt, the April 24, concert which consisted of a performance of Verdi's Requiem to celebrate Keith Smith's seventieth birthday. The choir was once again the Leicester Philharmonic, of which Keith Smith had been chorus master for eighteen years from 1972 to 1990.

Many former members of both the LSO and the Phil were invited back for this special event and the result was a huge orchestra and choir. Happily, this was matched by an equally large

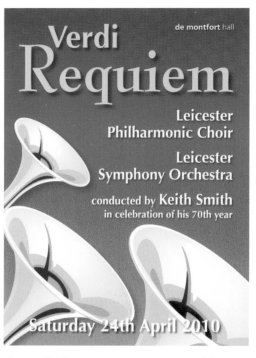

de montfort hall

Verdi Requiem

Leicester Philharmonic Choir

Leicester Symphony Orchestra

conducted by **Keith Smith**
in celebration of his 70th year

Saturday 24th April 2010

Cover of LSO concert programme, April 2010.

audience, which gave Keith a resounding ovation both before and after the performance.

At the reception following the concert many players and singers said how much they had enjoyed working again with Keith and that the concert brought back many happy memories. It was also a happy time for Keith who, as the LSO's conductor emeritus, continued to take an interest in the orchestra's affairs. Although this was his first appearance as conductor since his resignation in 1995, it was hoped that he would be invited back again in the not too distant future.

The performance, with soloists Denise Leigh, Amy Payne, Philip Cartwright and Sion Goronwy, was a fine one and drew

PHOTO: COURTESY OF PAUL COLE

LSO and LPC stand to take applause from the thousand strong audience. Verdi's Requiem is conducted by Keith Smith on April 24, 2010.

glowing praise from Peter Collett writing in the Leicester Mercury and from critics from further afield who had travelled to Leicester for the event.

Over the late May Bank Holiday of 2010, the orchestra went on tour, this time at the invitation of the Leicester and Strasbourg twinning associations as part of a series of events to celebrate half a century of twinning between the two cities. The LSO spent six days in Strasbourg and gave two concerts and the players were the guests of honour at a civic reception and were also treated to specially arranged sightseeing trips.

The concerts were conducted by Roland Melia and the orchestra was led by Catherine Cole. The first was held in Marmoutier Abbey and the second in Strasbourg's Eglise St Paul. The programme in each case included two choral works by Faure; Cantique de Jean Racine and four movements from the Requiem. The first concert also included Warlock's Capriol Suite, Nicolai's Overture to The Merry Wives of Windsor, MacCunn's Land of the Mountain and the Flood, and ended with Dvorak's 8th Slavonic Dance. The second also featured the Capriol Suite but the second half was taken up with Dvorak's New World Symphony. The orchestra was joined by a leading local choir, Les Petits Chanteurs de Strasbourg. Both concerts were very well received and attracted capacity audiences.

A member of the orchestra wrote: "We in Leicester are very lucky to be twinned with such a beautiful and fascinating city. The tour was a huge success. The orchestra was quite

PHOTO: COURTESY OF JOHN HOLLINS

Les Petits Chanteurs de Strasbourg (The Little Singers) with LSO outside Eglise St Paul on June 1, 2010.

PHOTO: COURTESY OF JEREMY OAKLEY

Concert publicity taped to the church door.

overwhelmed by the hospitality given to it in Strasbourg and all the time and effort which they had put into organising the two concerts for us."

The orchestra had the opportunity to reciprocate in July 2010 when they played host to Les Petits Chanteurs de Strasbourg and joined together in a concert at Leicester's Fraser Noble Hall, which included the Faure items along with the Merry Wives of Windsor Overture and the New World Symphony. Once again the conductor was the LSO's former musical director, Roland Melia.

The young Strasbourg choir was taken on a guided walk of Leicester and was given a civic reception in the Town Hall hosted by the Lord Mayor and Lady Mayoress of Leicester. Later in the day they sang in St Peter's Square, Highcross, Leicester and took part in a concert entitled Three Nations One Voice at Judgemeadow Community College. This event also included performances from Judgemeadow pupils and a German school exchange group, giving it a truly international flavour.

Both the orchestra's tour and the choir's visit to Leicester were supported financially and practically by the Leicester and Strasbourg twinning associations and both were considered a great success and enjoyed by everyone involved.

John Andrews made a return visit in November 2010 to conduct the opening concert of the LSO's 88th season. Spirit of the Dance was the title and it included and extra visual element: seventy six dancers from the Anne Oliver Stage School and the Leicester College of Performing Arts. The music included works by Delibes, Khachaturian, Tchaikovsky, Bernstein, Arnold and Borodin.

The Spirit of the Dance' concert, held on November 13, 2010 at De Montfort Hall.

Conductor Roland Melia with LSO on the steps of Eglise St Paul on June 1, 2010.

Once again, an imaginative programme attracted a good audience, bringing in new listeners, many of whom were related to the young dancers. The critic described the concert as "a feast for eyes and ears". The concert ended with Borodin's Polovtsian Dances, which "demonstrated beauty and drama in performance of both dance and music. John Andrews drew a crisp and lively performance from the orchestra."

Reiner Hersch was back for his third LSO concert on February 12 2011; this time the title was The Last Night of the Proms...Ever and as before, it was given as part of the Leicester Comedy Festival. The idea was to "rip off, poke fun at and generally ruin that jewel of the British concert season, The Last Night of the Proms. The by now customary large turnout heard "a superb concert with a great atmosphere, bursting with popular classics and a rousing finale of all the Proms favourites".

Critic John Dilleigh enjoyed the performance and his review contained these lines: "Hersch has been compared to Victor Borge and Gerard Hoffnung and, in demonstrating the similarities between a didgeridoo and a vacuum cleaner pipe, one can see why.

"The Leicester Symphony Orchestra fully entered into the spirit of the evening, playing with style and panache throughout, but particularly in Ronald Binge's Elizabethan Serenade and Puccini's Humming Chorus where they played – and hummed!" The concert was repeated at

Publicity for the The Battle of the Somme concert, November 12, 2011.

Stourbridge Town Hall on Saturday February 19, as a charity concert for the RNLI where it went down a storm to a packed house.

The LSO's interest in the music of Elgar continued on May 21, 2011 with a fine performance of Polonia, a rarely heard tone poem written in support of Poland during the First World War. The inclusion of this item in the programme was supported by a grant from the Elgar Society. It is a substantial work, and although based on Polish national tunes and themes by Chopin and Paderewski, every bar has the composer's musical personality stamped on it. It was thought that this was very likely to be the first performance in Leicester since Sargent's day. The Mercury's critic thought it was very enjoyable and "well worth the orchestra's time in preparing the splendid performance which was vigorous, dynamic and passionate". He added: "Guest conductor Jacques Cohen clearly revelled in the rich sonorities of orchestra and organ."

So captivatingly sad and sobering

A CONCERT of music influenced by the First World War began with George Butterworth's Banks of Green Willow; a performance with some lovely moments including a delicate flute and harp passage. By the exquisite closing of the piece it felt as though the orchestra had reached their comfort zone.

The first movement of Ravel's Le Tombeau de Couperin swirled and bubbled delightfully, having a good sense of line and emotion. The Forlane had a trance-like quality, the Menuet flowed gracefully. The Rigaudon danced with spirit.

Leicester Symphony Orchestra; Conductor – Levon Parikian
De Montfort Hall, Leicester
Review by Peter Collett

A fascinating pre concert talk by Imperial War museum historian Dr Toby Haggith and composer Laura Rossi had charted the restoration of the film The Battle of the Somme and the composition of a new score.

The film itself proved to be superbly restored and Rossi's score was captivating, conveying the mood of the film to perfection. It brought to life the expectant marching troops, preparations for battle, shelling of enemy lines, scenes of fighting and the grim reality of wounding and death.

From excitement to industry, perfectly timed gunfire, to sadness and despair, the music complemented the film in a seamless and atmospheric accompaniment which became one with the moving images.

The orchestra gave a stunning performance and had clearly put a lot of effort into ensuring this was the star of the evening.

A sobering, artistic end to the eve of Remembrance Sunday!

+

Leicester Mercury review of November 2011 concert.

Elgar wrote a number of patriotic works during the Great War in support of England, Belgium, France and Poland. The war itself devastated the composer and he never really got over it. Life had changed forever and this was reflected in his sombre and deeply-felt Cello Concerto, which was also played at this concert, with David Cohen as the soloist. He gave a superb performance that brought out the haunted introspection with exquisite phrasing and compelling musical insight.

Neil Roberts' guest at the well-attended pre-concert talk was Barry Collett, a leading Elgar expert, who as the founder conductor of the Rutland Sinfonia, made a pioneering recording of Elgar's War Music

LSO conductor John Andrews in 2012.

which is an invaluable document for Elgar scholars. Collett was awarded the Elgar Medal (the Elgar Society's highest honour) in 2011 for his services to the composer's lesser-known works.

The concert concluded with the Symphony No.3 for organ and orchestra by Saint-Saens; a work the LSO has programmed on a number of occasions in the past but seldom before with such panache. Peter Weston was the organist and interestingly, the versatile Barry Collett (who is also an expert on Saint-Saens) was one of the two pianists in this performance, which, with Cohen's broad pacing and meticulous attention to texture and detail, was far from routine.

Levon Parikian was in charge for the first concert of the 2011-2012 season. The programming was appropriate and another indication of the enterprising attitude of the LSO's management in the twenty first century. The date was Saturday November 12, and the theme of the concert was Remembrance. Each of the works played had an association with the Great War. The evening opened with the elegiac tone poem The Banks of Green Willow by George Butterworth, a promising young English composer, born in 1885 and killed in action in France in 1916. This was followed by Ravel's Tombeau de Couperin in which the movements are dedicated to friends who fought in the same conflict. After the interval the orchestra played Laura Rossi's memorable new score to the famous 1916 silent film Battle of the Somme as it was being shown.

Laura Rossi had been commissioned by the Imperial War Museum to write the score and Michael Beek writing in Music From the Movies described it as a powerful score which "very adeptly creates an emotional picture through impressive orchestral writing which is at once colourful, honourable, celebratory and moving".

Peter Collett writing in the Leicester Mercury thought the event was both memorable and

Conductor Roland Melia with LSO on the steps of Eglise St Paul on June 1, 2010.

moving. He had high praise for the playing of the orchestra – especially in the film score, which he found remarkably effective. The concert was prefaced by a discussion between Laura Rossi and Dr Toby Haggith of the Imperial War Museum. It is interesting to note that Levon's father Manoug Parikian, the then leader of London's Philharmonia Orchestra, had played the Beethoven Violin Concerto with the LSO back in February 1969.

The first work the LSO played in 2012, on February 18, was Holst's ballet suite, The Perfect Fool. It was given powerful reading that took a little while to ignite, but blazed once it did. The Mercury's critic was impressed with the steady but incisive tread and powerful building of climaxes. On the rostrum was the LSO's newly appointed conductor, John Andrews. He was known to the orchestra through his previous guest appearances and was a popular choice for the top job.

Andrews proved himself a good accompanist in the direct and unaffected performance of Bruch's G minor Violin Concerto with locally based violinist David Le Page as soloist. The concert ended with a performance of Berlioz's Symphonie Fantastique, which like the Holst, took a while to catch fire, but improved as it progressed and by the final two movements was "breathtaking" in its sonority and dramatic intensity.

John Andrews comes to the LSO with a wealth of experience in various fields. Since winning the special Orchestra Prize at the Bela Bartok Opera Conducting Competition in 2005, and completing his doctorate at Cambridge in 2007, he has been in demand for his musical fluency, passion and skill. Alongside his appointment with the LSO, Andrews is Music Director of the Stanley Hall Opera, Chorus Master of the renowned Norfolk and Norwich Festival and Principal Conductor of the Thames Youth Orchestra. He has also made a number of appearances with the English Touring Opera, English Chamber Opera and Pop-Up Opera. He is a resident conductor for City Music Services for whom he has conducted at Sadlers Wells and Glyndebourne and his current concert schedule includes appearances with the English Symphony Orchestra.

The season's final concert, on April 28, saw guest conductor Toby Purser take over the baton for a programme that began with Elgar's Froissart Overture and ended with Dvorak's 8th Symphony. In between came a selection of vocal and orchestral items from Carmen and songs by Delibes, Massenet and Rachmaninov. The evening made quite an impact, prompting Neil Roberts to write:

"The last concert of the season was something of a surprise. Right from the beginning in Elgar's Froissart Overture, a work that can sound very long winded, under Toby Purser the orchestra played with a confidence that for this listener has been too rarely present in recent seasons. Gone was the sense of prime aim, of the strings in particular, in being successful in the negotiation of difficulties. In its place was a real performance in which episodes were fully shaped. This feel of real music making carried over into the performance of operatic arias by Denise Leigh...her generous personality as an artist shone through and she fully deserved her ovation.

"However, it was the performance of Dvorak's 8th that was the revelation. Right from the beginning, with the strings digging in and really giving it some elbow, the performance took flight. In addition, as is vital with Dvorak, there were numerous incidental delights from the woodwind and the brass was incisive throughout. One felt under Purser's inspiring direction the full force of the symphonic argument and was able to forget completely that the LSO was an amateur orchestra. Clearly they loved working with this conductor and one hopes he will be enticed back."

The season ended with what is now a regular event for the LSO, a foreign tour. The destination was Paris and the tour took place over the Queen's Jubilee Bank Holiday weekend, beginning on Saturday June 2, and returning to Leicester on Thursday the 7th. The orchestra was flying the flag for Leicester and its first concert, on Monday June 3, was in the great Church of the Madeleine in the heart of the city. The guest conductor was Levon Parikian and the soloist was Eva Ganizate. The programme opened with Elgar's Froissart Overture and this was followed by a group of songs with orchestral accompaniment by Delibes, Massenet and Rachmaninov along with excerpts from Bizet's Carmen. The final item was Dvorak's 8th Symphony.

With a resonance of seven seconds, the acoustic of the vast church proved a challenge in rehearsal, but thanks to Parikian's careful direction and the orchestra's attentiveness, the performances did not suffer and were received extremely enthusiastically by a huge audience.

The second concert of the tour was held in Compiegne where the orchestra played the same programme with the addition of Mozart's Ave Verum which was played movingly on the oboe d'amore by the orchestra's principal oboist, Christine Griggs. As in the first concert,

Dame Evelyn Glennie in concert with LSO November 2012

Eva Ganizate performed the songs superbly. The concert ended with a protracted standing ovation and the members of the orchestra were feted by the citizens of Compiegne who gave them a marvellous welcome. They opened up the Chateau (normally closed Tuesdays) and provided guides who volunteered to show the players round on their day off. They also gave the LSO a magnificent lunch in the abbey and a reception with a supper in the Town Hall.

The tour provided plenty of time for sightseeing and one regular on the LSO's tours described it as "probably the best yet".

This tour was the seventh organised by LSO. Pat Dobson explained, "The tours are open to players, family members and friends. The hard work involved in organising is more than repaid by the benefit to the orchestra and the amount of enjoyment players and their supporters get. We usually play two concerts but we always allow plenty of time for sightseeing and relaxation. It is lovely to be able to have time for socialising - in normal rehearsals there is surprisingly little time for this. It really does help to build team spirit and at the same time we are proud to be flying the flag for Leicester." For three of the tours the orchestra received very valuable assistance from the Leicester Twinning Association, both financially and in terms of planning. These were for the visits to Krefeld and Strasbourg (twice), Leicester's twin cities.

Pat Dobson, John Andrews and Catherine Cole, in turn, the current chair, conductor and leader of LSO.

The 90th birthday season started in great style on November 10, 2012 with a very special celebratory Gala Evening with Dame Evelyn Glennie. This was a superb occasion

LEICESTER SYMPHONY ORCHESTRA

PRESIDENT	Michael Berkeley
HON. LIFE VICE-PRESIDENTS	Robert Meikle
HON. LIFE MEMBERS	Martin Gilding, George Middleton, Mike Riley, Arthur Temple, Graham Tomkinson, Terry Weston
CONDUCTOR EMERITUS	Keith Smith
CHAIRPERSON	Pat Dobson

First Violins
Philip Baker
Richard Bartholomew
Catherine Cole *
Molly Cummins
Alison Dovey
Brian Evans
Peter Handford
Cat Illingworth
Cat Ling
Richard Mee
Sarah Motson
Sarah Sharman
Alison Shelton
John Wakefield
Claire Walton

Second Violins
Suzie Alleyne
Rebecca Barrowcliffe
Jill Bentley
Helen Butterfield
Lois Clark
Sue Ford
Bernice Horn
Nicola Jackson
Ann Manley
Tom McClure
Jeremy Oakley
Roy Print
Lexie Rudd
Jill Rupp*
Nicola Veall
Carolyn Winkless

Violas
Thelma Bull
Hazel Carlin
Jane Dhonau
Liz Gotts
Natasha Haddock *
Gill Hadland
Caroline Roberts

Cellos
John Adams
Vaux Cairns
Anne Dixon
Pat Dobson *
Jenny Hand
Judith Lord
Richard Lord
Kumar Ramnarine
Malcolm Roe

Double Basses
Tim Batchelar
Peter Betts
Heather Hewitt
Lucy Keller
Ruth Porteous
Graham Tomkinson *

Flutes
Ailsa Gillies-Loach
Karen Hardy *
Mike Manley

Piccolo
Ailsa Gillies-Loach

Oboes
Christine Griggs *
Sarah Lindon
Daniel Saunders

Cor Anglais
Daniel Saunders

Clarinets
Paul Gray *
Robert Greenlees *
Sue Thompson

Bass Clarinet
Robert Greenlees

Bassoons
Karen Goss
Shelagh Thomson *

Horns
Julian Haslam
Nigel Moore *
Vicki Reynolds
Sarah Tyler

Trumpets
Andy MacFarlane *
Matt McLavy
Mark Needham
Nick Smith

Trombones
John Gornall *
Richard Siddons

Bass Trombone
Alan Griggs

Tuba
Terry Weston

Timpani
Ariel Zaviezo

Percussion
Debbie James
Paloma Maldonado
Hugh McLaren
Derek Scurll

Keyboard
Marguerite Beatson

* Section Principal

Front of House: Jill Bloomfield, Val Green, Aubrey Green

Programme: Mike Lord
Programme graphic design and printing: Ask Sue Witts Printing Services

LSO player list November 2012.

where a huge audience was treated to a wide range of music which naturally included Sargent's An Impression on a Windy Day, the piece with which he launched his career back in 1921. Alongside this was the premier of a new piece of music, Jonathan Ostlund's Celebration Fanfare and Procession, which was the winner of a composition competition that LSO had run to celebrate their ninetieth anniversary.

17. Summing Up and Looking Forward

When the Leicester Symphony Orchestra was created there were those who predicted its demise almost before it had given its first concert. It was, they felt, an unnecessary addition to an already crowded classical music scene and it would not win enough support to survive. But ninety years on it is flourishing, with an inspiring young conductor at its head and a dynamic and far-sighted Council of Management. The orchestra celebrates its ninetieth birthday season with well-founded optimism and a strong sense of identity. It is well established at the heart of local music making and looks forward to its centenary with confidence and enthusiasm.

Pat Dobson who has served on the Council of Management since 1989 and chaired the orchestra since 1997, writes:

"I feel it is a great honour to be so actively involved in such am amazing organisation. I receive great support from the Council of Management. In particular, Jenny Hand and Nicola Veall deserve special mention for their unstinting high quality work over many years. I am also carried along by the sheer enthusiasm and dedication of the players, not to mention all the other volunteers who give their time and expertise to help in the running of the orchestra.

"We look back over ninety years to a different world. Long gone are the days of special trains and buses to concerts, with audiences of 2,500. But that was before broadcasting, before recorded music and before the advent of talking cinema let alone television and the internet. Today there is an almost infinite variety of forms of entertainment and therefore the Leicester Symphony Orchestra has to fight hard to attract audiences.

We have a fascinating history and one thing it shows us is that nothing is sure. There have been times when its survival was in doubt but it has weathered the storms and LSO is now very much alive and well and holding its own in these difficult economic times. We look forward to continuing to attract new members, and have a healthy balance of young players in the orchestra as well as a core of loyal older members.

It is important to note that the orchestra receives no subsidies from the public purse, it is wholly self-funded with monies coming from ticket sales, membership subscriptions and occasional donations. LSO is made up of talented local musicians and nobody is paid apart from our conductor and soloists. We are amateur in the true sense of the word – we do it for love, the love of music.

In recent years we have been greatly privileged to work with many talented professionals,

Current LSO members with thirty or more years' service. For each, the date of joining LSO is given. They are:

Back row, left to right: Paul Gray, clarinet, 1976; Thelma Bull, viola, 1972 then regularly from 1982; Robert Greenlees, clarinet, 1973; Graham Tomkinson, double bass, 1963; John Wakefield, violin, 1982; Brian Evans, violin, 1977 and Caroline Roberts (née Smith),viola, 1974.

Front row, left to right: Terry Weston, tuba, 1965; Malcolm Roe, cello, 1974; Pat Dobson, cello, 1982; Karen Hardy, flute, 1982 and Roy Print, violin, 1979.

Shelagh Thomson (not on the photo), originally violin and now bassoon, has given over thirty years' service from 1979.

amongst whom are Nicholas Daniel and Dame Evelyn Glennie. Both have well established international reputations and are keen to support the orchestra and this book. Their commendations are given on the back cover.

My last word must go to you, the audience. Your loyal support over the years is greatly appreciated. Thank you. To those who have never been to one of our concerts, I say come. Not because we have a long and fascinating history, but because we have something very positive to offer and we are proud of what we do. We do things well and look forward to many more years of great music-making."

The Author

Neil Crutchley was born in Leicester where his love of music was encouraged at the Gateway School and his local church choir. He attended his first Leicester Symphony Orchestra concert as a schoolboy in 1967 and has been writing the orchestra's programme notes since 1983. He was the classical music correspondent of the Leicester Mercury from 1984 to 2012, during which time he wrote appoximately 1,500 concert reviews and more than a thousand weekly music features. He was a member of staff at Leicester's Goldsmith Music and Drama Library from 1971 to 1997 and was for a number of years choirmaster at Harrison Road Methodist Church, Leicester and lecturer in music appreciation at the city's Adult Education College. He continues to write and lecture on music and local history and is the president of the Leicester Recorded Music Society.

PHOTO: COURTESY OF JOHN HOLLINS

The illustrations have been selected by Sam Dobson, a long-time supporter of the LSO, mostly from the orchestra's own archive. Where they have been provided by others, acknowledgement is given. "I hope these give a flavour of the archive. It has been a great privilege to have access to these invaluable records. The LSO's archive is by no means complete and if anyone has any material which could help to complete the picture, we would be very interested. Please contact us through our website: www.leicestersymphonyorchestra.co.uk"

Index

Appendix 1:

LSO Dates at a Glance

1922   LSO founded – first concert 24 October

1923   Mary Thornley (nee Ashmell) joined aged 14, first concert April

1924   First performance in Leicester of Beethoven's 9th symphony

1925   First performance in Leicester of Elgar's Cello Concerto

1933   Sargent's 2 year illness led to amalgamation with Leicester Philharmonic Society

1937   LSO separates from LPS

1941   LSO under title of People's Concert, conductor Arthur Thornley, leader Mary Thornley

1942   Sargent's last known LSO concert 12 July

1943   Grace Burrow's last known concert as LSO leader 2 May

1948   Doreen Adnett, nee Robinson, joined LSO (unconfirmed date)

1949   Harry Shaw appointed conductor

1950   Mary Thornley appointed leader

1959   Simeon Iliffe appointed conductor

1963   LSO records soundtrack to film "City of Contrasts"

1967   Sargent dies 3 October

1972   Simeon Iliffe's last LSO concert

1974   Keith Smith appointed conductor

1978   Anne Gosling (now Tupling) joins LSO, leader May 1983 to April 1994

1980   Sargent and the LSO, First Day Cover Stamp issue

1983   Mary Thornley retires as leader

1992   Mary Thornley's last LSO concert November

1995   Keith Smith's last LSO concert May

1995   Doreen Adnett, leader from November until November 2003

1996   Roland Melia guest conductor November, appointed conductor 1997

1999   Ghent – LSO's first overseas tour, with Roland Melia

2001   Nicholas Daniel guest conductor May, appointed conductor 2002

2002   Pavel Kotla conducts LSO for the first time, February

2002   Strasbourg/Offenburg tour with Nicholas Daniel

2004   Paris tour with Nicholas Daniel

2004   Mike Shaw appointed leader for November, his last concert February 2009

2005   Nicholas Daniel's last concert, with Dame Evelyn Glennie, November

2005   Krefeld/Aachen tour with new conductor Pavel Kotla, his last concert was June 2009

2007   John Andrews' guest conductor, March

2007   Catherine Cole, nee Axcell's, first concert, November, appointed leader, June 2009

2008   Doreen Adnett's last concert, April

2008   Poland & Czech Republic tour with Pavel Kotla

2010   Strasbourg/Marmoutier tour with Roland Melia

2011   John Andrews appointed conductor

2012   Paris/Compiegne tour with guest conductor Levon Parikian

2012   90th anniversary gala evening with Dame Evelyn Glennie

Appendix 2:

Overseas tours

Strasbourg 2002

Ghent 1999

Krefeld 2006

Paris 2004

Poland 2008